Growing Up
HAUNTED

A Ghostly Memoir

Alexandra Holzer

Forewords by **Dr. Hans Holzer**
and Countess Catherine Buxhoeveden

4880 Lower Valley Road, Atglen, Pennsylvania 19310

DEDICATION

I dedicate this novel to all those in my life, to those reading this novel, those in the afterlife and life itself.

Life is meant to be lived, cherished and enjoyed as best as possible.

Schiffer Books are available at special discounts for bulk purchases for sales promotions or premiums. Special editions, including personalized covers, corporate imprints, and excerpts can be created in large quantities for special needs. For more information contact the publisher:

Published by Schiffer Publishing Ltd.
4880 Lower Valley Road
Atglen, PA 19310
Phone: (610) 593-1777; Fax: (610) 593-2002
E-mail: Info@schifferbooks.com

For the largest selection of fine reference books on this and related subjects,
please visit our web site at **www.schifferbooks.com**
We are always looking for people to write books on new and related subjects. If you have an idea for a book please contact us at the above address.

This book may be purchased from the publisher.
Include $3.95 for shipping.
Please try your bookstore first.
You may write for a free catalog.

In Europe, Schiffer books are distributed by
Bushwood Books
6 Marksbury Ave.
Kew Gardens
Surrey TW9 4JF England
Phone: 44 (0) 20 8392-8585; Fax: 44 (0) 20 8392-9876
E-mail: info@bushwoodbooks.co.uk
Website: www.bushwoodbooks.co.uk
Free postage in the U.K., Europe; air mail at cost.

Other Schiffer Books on Related Subjects
Danny's Bed, 978-0-7643-2703-2, $9.95
The Dead Won't Hurt You...Or Will They?, 0-7643-1701-6, $16.95
Please go to Schiffer Publishing's web site for more great titles relating to ghosts and the supernatural.

Copyright © 2008 by Alexandra Holzer
Library of Congress Control Number: 2007940474

Design Concept by Alexandra Holzer
Cover Design by Schiffer Publishing Designer, Bruce Waters
Book Designed by Mark David Bowyer
Type set in Piano Bold / Humanist521 BT

ISBN: 978-0-7643-2895-4
Printed in China

CONTENTS

Acknowledgments

I thank first and foremost, Hans and Catherine, whose lives has paved the path that I am walking.

I thank my four children for the continuos reminder that many worlds can exist and magic could be real. And, I thank my spouse for his continued support during my craziness when the "mad typist" was at work.

I thank all of my supportive family and friends in believing my visions, and my publisher and their team, for allowing me the opportunity to see this project become a reality.

Finally, I acknowledge the supernatural and believe there is such a word called fate and what is meant to be...shall be.

Forewords

I am pleased to see that my youngest daughter has also become a writer and a good one at that. But, I am not surprised because we are very close in this family. She has inherited my so-called talent. At any rate, I am pleased that she is doing well as a writer and I recommend her work to anyone. I am thrilled to see her talent show so well and so unusually as I wish her the best with all her future successes.

—Professor Dr. Hans Holzer,
Parapsychologist and Author

When my daughter Alexandra told me she was planning to write a memoir of her father and I, I was surprised to say the least. That was a big task taking into account the magnitude of information and history. Her father, a known parapsychologist and writer, and mother, an artist and career woman with a rich historical background, whose "entry to this world" was at the outbreak of World War II.

"It is going to be a light to medium memoir, not a detailed type of book," Alex said to me.

Starting with the two meshing together and working as a team, the first book published was *Ghost Hunter*. I worked closely with Hans for ten years in the investigations and ultimately illustrated many of these books in pen and that led to paintings of haunted houses and many art exhibits in conjunction with the books. (I can't wait to) see the final results of *Growing Up Haunted*.

—Countess Catherine Buxhoeveden

Introduction

What does one say about their family when growing up? Well, it's a sticky situation no matter how you slice it. For myself, I have always been and still remain very candid and true in my remarks of 'the family,' but there are many who do not feel comfortable speaking of such things. In some families it may even be considered taboo to do just that. With keeping the respect factor and feelings in check, I am able to speak openly of such touchy subjects that may or may not cross the line. Eggshell walking for me is cracking all the eggs along the way.

What juicy bit of detail can I, the daughter of this famous pioneering 145-titles carrying author, give you to start with as an appetizer? How about the time when my parents were still married and on good living terms hosting their New Year's Eve parties? Now there's an interesting place to start with where I can pick up my memories. I can still remember this odd woman who peered over me offering me a bit of her herbal tea. I had a bit of a cold and so at the ripe old age of six, knew even back then to politely say, "no, thank you" and graciously walk away. I actually ran and hid behind my mother, but you get my point. Good manners and politeness was very important in this family. Or, I can start with the beautiful Upper West Side six-bedroom apartment itself and the strange goings on there.

However, before we begin that whole episode, there's just one more item I'd like to mention first. Some of you already know Hans' background as a writer, but what I am here to enlighten all of you on is how he got started, where he went, and how he ended up. Along the way I describe the fated path he and my mother were pre-destined to be on. I truly believe they were brought together to create this paranormal understanding and awareness in the public at a time of huge skepticism and mistruth's on the topic itself.

Most of you don't realize Catherine's background, and that she was brave and confident enough to openly admit that things did exist throughout our lives. My grandmother's childhood and marriage to my grandfather will shed a much exciting, historical, and, at times, disheartening light.

I was interviewed by a man who turned to ghost-hunting and paranormal investigations due mainly to Hans' career. As a result, this man formed his own society in Pennsylvania. He grew up with his own ghostly encounters and couldn't believe that there was a person actually seeking out the dead. That person was Hans Holzer and he was their hero. Hans blazed into any house, castle, barn, cemetery, woods, apartment, or tavern … and anything else you can think of and got right down to business. His mediums were usually women who were not young at the time. Sometimes a photographer would accompany them, but on most cases, it was just Hans and an elderly famed medium brought along to help translate.

As Hans aged, his mediums tended to get younger. Very clever, I thought to myself, clever indeed that sly dog. I still think they should come out with a new super hero character with a white cape called 'Ghost Man.' No house too haunted, no ghost too scary, Ghost Man is on the job and will even knock over the fairies. An annoying fact is that we as a society in the 1960s still wanted to simply explain away unseen forces at work. Instead rock and roll prevailed, socialites and huge parties drowned out the haunted nights of Manhattan. New York ghosts (the loudest of them all, thank goodness) found a way to still be heard and knew Hans was on his way to do just that. I am reminded of one of my favorite lines from the movie "Mrs. Doubtfire" with Robin Williams. The scene where Mrs. Doubtfire is screaming in her muddled British accent, "Help is on the wayyyyyy!" in the restaurant scene. That was Hans, but his get up was a black raincoat, a 1940s Hollywood detective-style hat, and a crew of mediums and photographers on his tail. He changed the perception of the unexplained by showing how to confront and accept them. Hans and Catherine added to the literary and art world by creating an interest, passion, and understanding in looking at life in a new way. Through the wise hollow eyes of the afterlife, Hans became their mortal interpreter.

Hans and Catherine had two children who, too, were on a fated pre-destined path. Now, at this point in my life, I get it and what it should be for myself — following in my father's deeply ghosted footsteps as a writer and artist. As for the other Holzer sibling, she went the way of the volleyball, and to this day none of us can figure out where in the world she got that talent. Catherine was good at sports, but not the way my sister was. Hans never met a tennis racket that he liked! He'd always argue with the plastic wired oval racket and end up entangled in the net. He of course was the victor and the racket and net stood hanging off one another in great defeat and despair. When I played on my school's basketball team, I was nicknamed, 'Wrong Way Holzer,' as I was a great shooter for the OTHER team. Oh well, such is life!

I hope to provide you with an understanding of Hans' accomplishments, as they are only one small piece of a whole puzzle. I hope to put together for you a beginning, middle, and no end — and by "no end" I mean I want to leave you with an impression of a detailed picture that hopefully will hang in your minds for a while. For Catherine, we look to a larger piece of history and the Russian culture that laid the foundation of her birth. There was much greatness and nobility in her family; many were honored and decorated who fought gallantly to preserve our way of life. The paranormal, the afterlife, our angelic guides, and family members were all with us way back then, and some still remain as we continue to serve our purpose on this plane of existence we call earth. Hence I believe in the purpose of my parents.

The Royal Russian Count was a man named Alexander Buxhoeveden. No, he wasn't a count like Dracula although he did move his new bride and children into a haunted castle way up on a hill in Italy, and he did have a heavy thick Russian accent and wore dark blazers and a cloak. Well, no, not really a cloak, but I would like to believe he did. Rosine Claire Vidal joined Alexander Buxhoeveden in marriage and bore five children. Since Alexander already had five from his first marriage, this was going to be a bumpy ride for Rosine. Two wars, loss of children, two husbands, and many grandchildren left her no peace in her soul. However, she persevered throughout her long existence, always with a smile on her face. Staying a very spiritual woman, Rosine was in a quest for knowledge of life and death. She and Hans got along famously when Catherine introduced the two as future in-laws. To my sister and I, she was the best grandmother, endearingly termed Nana, and so began our journey with this fascinating woman from another time and place.

Chapter One:
HANS, THE GHOST HUNTER:
A BRIEF INTRODUCTORY

August 2007: "Interview with the Ghost Hunter"
by Dirk Vander Ploeg

We begin our look at Hans, the Ghost Hunter, with his most recent interview as he gives few and far nowadays. This interview was conducted by my editor at UFO Digest.com who has a deep appreciation and respect for Hans and what he stands for. He may not agree with everything Hans says — or doesn't say, but he allows him to answer the way only Hans could. Blunt, direct, to the point, somewhat offensive but informative and intelligent.

Synopsis

[Editor Dirk Vander Ploeg] had the opportunity to interview Mr. Hans Holzer, the internationally known writer, parapsychologist and university professor and father of Alexandra Holzer, a contributing writer to UFO Digest. Mr. Holzer has written over 140 books concerning ghosts, the paranormal, and UFOs. He is 87-years old and is publishing a new book. His mind is sharp and, as you'll read, his opinions are straightforward and direct. I appreciate the assistance of Alexandra Holzer, without whom these interviews would not have taken place.

During my initial interview with Holzer on Wednesday August 1, 2007, we discussed various subjects including ghosts, hauntings, and UFOs and their occupants. The following is based on my notes taken during that conversation.

Regarding the modern "ghost buster:" Holzer believes that they rely too heavily on gadgets and don't take the time to conduct the interviews and gather real evidence. He insists that any serious investigation must include the use of a proven medium or transmedium in order to make actual contact with the spirit or ghost.

Science and the paranormal: A scientist, Holzer said there really is no paranormal. There are just areas of "our reality that we don't have the ability to understand, but if we progress scientifically, we will eventually discover and recognize the complexities of our existence and understand that everything is part of the natural order of our universe."

Angels and religion: Holzer said that there were no angels and that all world religions were basically large companies and that scaring the "Hell" out of their followers was very profitable.

UFOs and their occupants: Holzer doesn't believe it's accurate to call extraterrestrials 'aliens.' "Aliens are from other countries, not star systems. A more accurate term would be extraterrestrial or humanoid." Does he believe that extraterrestrials altered our DNA thousands of years ago, as (scientist) Zecharia Sitchin suggests? Holzer agrees, "It is possible."

I asked Mr. Holzer why he believes that the ETs are abducting our citizens and his answer was both profound and frightening. First he thinks that abductees are being taken because the extraterrestrials are performing genetic experiments in an attempt to create a super-race of hybrids: Supermen! Then he added, "although they may be thousands if not millions of years older than us, and have mastered both telepathy and space-travel, they have lost their 'humanity,' and it is this loss that they are desperately trying to recover."

The following are answers to a set of follow-up questions to Mr. Holzer on August 12, 2007.

Questions and Answers

Editor: Can you give us your definition of what a ghost or haunting is?

Hans: Human beings die and when one sees a ghost, they are also seeing a spirit, which is where the confusion lies. When we are born, we are born with a double body, an etheric body. People see an inner body with a likeness to what that person looked like in life. It is hard to tell the difference sometimes, but this is a ghost. A spirit is the inner body that shows in the form called a ghost and is not satisfied and can't pass on. Thus, a haunting is this ghost in a place where it can't leave.

Editor: Could you explain what was the "Amityville Horror"?

Hans: I was invited there twice and was one of the first on the scene. The first book was written by another man whose editor actually wrote it. They wanted it more of a book about horror whereas my books were about the case and the investigations leading up to and after the murders. This was not a horror case to me. I looked at it differently and went on to write many books on this topic thereafter.

Editor: Of all of your investigations concerning ghosts and hauntings, which cases stand out in your mind? Which did you find to be the most interesting?

Hans: They are all equally to the same to me. People write or call me because they are scared or a place needs my help. Then, I would go and bring a well-trained transmedium and investigate.

Editor: Your investigations always involved the use of mediums. Could you tell us why?

Hans: A scientific investigation must have a well-trained transmedium for communication. It is the only way.

Editor: What is your opinion on today's "ghost busters" with their websites, radio and television shows that feature electronic voice phenomena, thermometers, voltage meters and so on?

Hans: Today's Ghost Busters, with their equipment, for me is all nonsense. You don't need any of this. To me, it is an amateur's way. I did it and succeeded just the same. It may not have been as exciting as today's reality shows that are broadcasting, but, I am the real deal and this is where I differ from all those out there currently and why I am the one who brought out more investigators interested in the subject itself.

Editor: You are the author of over 100 books and I understand you have just published a new book — *The Spirit Connection*. Could you tell us what the book is about?

Hans: *The Spirit Connection* shows cases where people came to me about receiving help from the 'Other Side.' Sometimes it is a relative or friend. The intervention by these people was best said by the late [Medium] Eileen Garrett, "Death is life's other door." A good friend of mine, Bishop Jim Pike, and I were taking a walk one day out in California. On this walk, we discussed his late son's recent communication with his father. Jim didn't know what to call his book about his story and so I came up with the name, 'The Other Side of Life.' From then on, many titles would become the 'other side this, the other side that' and so on.

Editor: Many people recognize your name, Hans Holzer, but associate you with ghosts. But you have written dozens of books about the paranormal and UFOs.

Hans: Yes, I am best known for writing about ghosts. So much so, that at one point back in the day, I came up with the idea to do a TV series on ghosts but it never 'materialized,' pardon the pun.

Editor: Do you believe we are being visited by extraterrestrials from other planets?

Hans: Yes. Since ancient times, I believe this, and the one case that has always led me is the Betty Hill case in which these beings were 37 1/2 light years away from a specific Sun, which is also a Star. Many other planets have life on their stars. It all varies on age and how far away they are in order to sustain life. Look, we haven't gotten there yet, so we really don't know. All we do know is the book, *Interrupted Journey*, which tells us in detail about stars and their suns existing where life can survive.

Editor: How many ET races are visiting the earth?

Hans: The universe is enormous. We just don't know. And there are no monsters in space, that's just Hollywood.

Editor: Why are they here?

Hans: As we investigate people here on our planet, they do the same with their kind and ours. They're called humanoids and it varies depending on conditions of life and distance of the planets to their suns/stars. We have no definite knowledge other than the exciting cases at hand, mainly Betty Hill.

Editor: Why are they abducting humans?

Hans: They want to learn about us in our system. With those who are not returned, I believe they are kept for research. As they have their own doctors, are curious about us, as we would be of them.

Editor: I understand you regressed or had someone regress Betty Hill and helped her recover the memory of the famous Starmap. Could you tell us your experience with Betty and Barney Hill?

Hans: Betty Hill, I knew very well as you probably already know. She told me that the captain of the ship asked her to show them where she came from. Betty had asked the captain where she was and he told her to answer her first. She replied that she was only a housewife, what did she really know? Not content with the answer, the captain turned away and pushed her back and told her that he would not tell her where she was. Barney had passed before I had a chance to meet him.

Editor: There seems to be a new religion emerging that combines extraterrestrials, with their messages concerning nuclear annihilation, over-population and global warming.

Hans: Religion has nothing to do with space. Global warning, well yes, that may be so. Other life is worried about how we are on earth because it will affect their systems setting off a possible chain reaction. I believe they are trying to protect themselves.

Editor: Believers are relating ETs to angels, seeing the grays as messengers.

Hans: Angels are a fantasy part of religion. They want to be called, 'Beings of Light.' And ETs are NOT Beings of Light.

Editor: What is your opinion about mixing UFOs with religion?

Hans: UFOs come from other suns/stars where there is no religion involved.

Editor: In your opinion does the United States and other governments have knowledge of the extraterrestrials and their craft visiting our planet?

Hans: Yes. I believe the British and our government and others know about them.

Editor: If so, why do they not disclose this information to the public?

Hans: Because they do not want to frighten the public as I feel we are not ready.

Editor: Why do many abductees report seeing agents of the C.I.A. and other government agencies on the ships or in the operating rooms during alien abductions?

Hans: CIA, no. Perhaps part of the other ET's team looking similar to our kind, which I believe some do.

Chapter Two:

Notable cases

For All You Amityville Seekers

I would be remiss if I didn't include the Amityville 'Horror' case as being one of Hans' most notable cases — just for the sheer reason that Hans really was the authority on the topic. He was one of very few to get that call to come out to Long Island and investigate the property and inside the house. That also included going into the prison and having one-on-one conversations with the alleged murderer, which we still have the recordings of buried in that closet in his office (which I talk about later in this book).

To this day, as with any high profile, controversial murder cases, there will always be new twists and turns as if the house was still alive and people still perishing. He was there during a time that many during that era, and decades later, were not. That's all I can say about that. Sometimes, it is better that some things are left at the door. This being one of them. The loss of lives that day should be the only thing remembered and reflected upon. I think a better story and approach could be told in the future and perhaps Hans will have an opportunity in doing so. Hans never cared about what others thought about his findings. He was involved more than anyone else and was not running in a popularity contest. He was in it for all the right reasons, with his reputation in the business. This was just like any other case only the stakes were much higher. He knew and understood that and carefully went about it.

The book, *Murder in Amityville*, came out in 1978. The information was from a series of works about Amityville. Some jumped on the band wagon while others tried profiting from the case in one way or another. Hans never made much off of his investigations with Amityville. To this day, he still has a place in the literary world on the topic re-releasing a large three volume book encompassing the beginning, middle and end. His original book was loosely adapted into the film, *Amityville: The Possession*. Then came this idea to do *The Amityville Murders* on television, further exposing the whole case years after it began. The never-aired TV documentary hosted by yours truly, parapsychologist Hans Holzer, was about the real life murders committed in Amityville, New York. On November 13, 1974, Ronald DeFeo killed his entire family in the house that would become "The Amityville Horror." It seems that the documentary couldn't build enough interest in any of the networks, so it was shelved. *The Amityville Murders* website claimed that it was "outstanding." This is true. There are two sides to a story and, in Hans' case, he had his. I will leave Amity to rest in peace as it is much deserved. I would like to see a great re-make of it though, from Hans' latest book. One never knows where our paths will lead us to next....

A Haunting in Wilmington

The explanations did not satisfy those who had seen the light. Some of the men said it could have been reflections from an automobile headlight while others claimed it was a haze that sometimes forms off a swamp. Numerous sightings of the light, however, predate the invention of the car! And the ominous glow didn't really resemble swamp haze or phosphorus gas, as it is scientifically called. Many newspapers and magazines, such as *Life*, were intrigued and pursued the ghostly occurrence, but to no avail. Drastic measures were finally taken in April of 1964. A German man by the name of Hans Holzer was called. Known as a professional 'ghost hunter' and the world's leading authority on ghosts, he was hired to solve the mystery and to bring closure to the Joe Baldwin saga. Joe Baldwin was a man that was killed on the train tracks and was said to have haunted the area until the tracks were removed. The Southeastern North Carolina Beach Association brought in Holzer, author of the book, *Ghost Hunter*.

Holzer was accompanied by his twenty-five year old wife Catherine Buxhoeveden-Holzer. Born in Merano, Italy at Castle Rovina, Countess Catherine Buxhoeveden is a direct descendent of Russia's Catherine the Great from an uninterrupted family line dating back to 880 AD. As Hans, was becoming a well-known author of many books on parapsychology, ghosts, and hauntings, Catherine traveled far and wide with him, assisting with research for his books and subsequently illustrating them in pen and ink. The supernatural intrigued her, and she had won an award in New York the previous year for her impressive paintings of ghosts and haunted houses. However, she attracted far more media attention as she was reputedly the great, great, great-granddaughter of Catherine the Great.

Catherine and Hans landed at New Hanover County Airport and received a tremendous welcome. The mayor, a band, many citizens of the area, and 1,000 New Hanover High School students carrying lighted lanterns were there to hail the arrival of Hans Holzer and his wife. Despite the big production made of his arrival, Hans came no closer to unraveling the enigma than anyone else did. A reporter with *The Wilmington Star News*, Charles Joyner, accompanied by a friend and both their wives, claimed they had all seen the light one night. Mr. Joyner even wrote about it, saying the glow spread three hundred yards, but lasted only a few minutes. It reappeared about forty minutes later, again lasting only a few minutes before disappearing for the rest of the night. According to reports gathered by many witnesses, there didn't appear to be any reason for the light. It was seen at different times of the year, as well as different times of night. Some soldiers from Fort Bragg claimed they had shot bullets at the light. But, while people continued to see the strange light, they gave up trying to figure it out. When Fort Bragg was closed and the tracks were taken up in 1977, the light disappeared. It has never been seen again. Hans said it was because Mr. Joe Baldwin had finally found his head and could now rest in peace. Parts of this story were taken from an article that appeared in a newspaper in New Hanover County, Wilmington. The mystery was one of many that would follow.

This is how it began...

Chapter Three:

Little Hans Holzer

When you start kindergarten – your very first year of elementary school – it's considered a pretty big deal. It can be exciting, exhilarating, happy, sad, or, in my father's case and the other children in his new class ... frightening! Little Hans, at age five, took kindergarten to a new level. The year was 1925 in Vienna, Austria, so you can imagine what it would have been like with the teachers and the strict rules they had in place.

Now I have put two of my children through the kindergarten process, and if they pulled any of the stunts Little Hans did in 1925 today in 2007, I'd be in the psychiatrist's office to explain why we see 'dead people.'

My father saw 'dead people' before the adorable actor Haley Joel Osment saw them. At the ripe old age of five, little Hans gathered up all the little chairs he could muster and summoned the children in his class to sit around him — he had some stories to tell. Kittens, puppy dogs, mice running up and down the clock, and an old woman in a shoe? Now that would be normal and probably deemed okay. Ghosts and haunted houses and people running amuck and in fear of their lives — yes, little Hans created a whole new meaning to 'story time.' As a result, he was sent home with enough pieces of paper about his strange and unacceptable behavior that he and grandfather Leonard began to decorate the walls in the house with it, thus saving on wallpapering.

What sort of person has a ghost child that comes in the form of a living person? Who did those from up above choose to have a child like this that exhibited such odd, unworldly behavior beyond his years to raise on this earth? They chose brave and "un-spookable" Leonard, a very sophisticated man of his times who came to America at age sixteen in 1903, but when he caught news of his sickly father back in Vienna, he left New York to go and take care of him until his passing. It was there in Vienna that Leonard would become a partner in the store his father left him. The shop was an elegant gentlemen's clothing store. When he met his future bride, Marta, Leonard had to travel three hours from Vienna to a town called Brenn in what is now called The Czech Republic so they could court one another.

Now that's love! I wonder if anyone out there still encounters these types of strong and true romances. I'd love to think so. But being that this is not a 'chick' story, I will get right off the topic in the next sentence:

Leonard and Marta Holzer had two sons, Kurt and then little Hans.

In 1928, at the age of eight, little Hans' Uncle Henry asked for a collection of poetry from my father, seeing his keen ability to already take to paper with pen in hand, and surprised him at Christmas with his first publication. At age fourteen, little Hans received his first newspaper assignment in which he was to travel to a palace in The Czech Republic and write about the antiques that were placed in a special room called 'The Porcelain Room.' This had many historical benefits to it, which little Hans devoured up right away. This opportunity eventually led to his desire to learn all there was to know about artifacts, history, and everything in-between. But it would not be pursued for a long time to come. Leonard, with his family, came back over to New York in 1938.

Kurt, being the eldest, moved from New York in 1942 to England; later on, he moved to California where he met his wife and had his own family. There he lived and passed away. His wife, my Aunt Liesel, is still out in California, and while she has very few possessions, she also has a lot because her heart and mind is filled with love despite all the difficult times in her life. I am proud to say we all still keep in touch and appreciate her.

When do we get to all those darn ghosts, you ask. Soon, soon... all good things come in time.

Hans had met my mother Catherine (*who will have her own chapter in this book for two good reasons: she had the guts to marry my father; and she too has quite an interesting background, which makes up half of this puzzle.*) Meeting at a party for the Kit Kat Club in Manhattan, a fancy place where cigarette ashes were as long as the cigarettes themselves and ladies' hair were thick and curled and unmovable. The men wore penguin suits and laughed half heartily as their drinks swirled around with the melting ice cubes. Hans attended this party with his date at the time, my late Aunt Rosemarie Buxhoeveden, my mother's sister. Well, needless to say Hans and Rosemarie decided it would be best to remain friends, which left room for him and Catherine to mingle.

When I first found out about this bit of detail, I was around sixteen years old. The thoughts that ran through my head! I was a bit disgusted to say the least. I was, even at that age, an old soul, so it just didn't sit well with me.

However, Hans and Catherine wed later that year and Rosemarie always remained in their lives as a wonderful sibling. Of course, Rosemarie too had many difficult moments and actually fled New York for California, where she had tried to commit suicide on two separate occasions. Hans and Catherine took her in at their New York City apartment, where she was able to witness the birth of the first Holzer daughter. After some time, she left again to live in San Francisco, where she would try to "find" herself. I think, after reading the personal letters she wrote to my mother during that time, that she never really did find herself. She sang in clubs, mingled with the boys and girls, and always seemed to have a positive disposition no matter what that day would bring her. She had healed herself to a degree, but just couldn't find her whole self. Eventually the very tall, slender, dark haired, blue eyed woman affectionately known as Aunt Mosie, or Aunt Mushy as I preferred to call her, would find herself with her true companion in life. Though her life would be tragically cut short by cancer.

But, she would come back two years later to push me to write again! I must say this: the dead are not so dead and boy do they talk a lot. But that is another chapter later on.

There was other heartbreak — Hans' mother Marta passed away, and for Catherine, her brother was killed, horribly, after his car went over the side of a bridge, plummeting to the dark cold waters below, never to return again. Catherine and her Parisian mother Rosine still haven't quite recouped from that, but have accepted that it was his fate.

It was in the early 1960s that Hans and Catherine took in Leonard, around the same time as the birth of my sister Nadine. Leonard hadn't lived there long when he too passed on.

He came back along with my late Aunt Mosie — and the two of them burned both ends of the spirit phones. I ended up with such a ghastly spirit bill and had no one to complain about it to. That's the problem with the other side — you just can't seem to get anyone when you need to. When you do get someone, it's obvious that they're so transparent!

Timing is everything in this life, as Hans and Catherine believed more and more on their travels investigating all walks of life experiencing the afterlife. Anyway, let's get to those who helped launch it all shall we?

Chapter Four:

Albert von Buxhoeveden

I'd like to give you some background on where Catherine came from so you have an idea of how grand her family really was and how she and Hans connected. We'll start with Albert von Buxhoeveden, whose life was described in the *Chronic of Livonia* written by Henry of Latvia: "Albert of Riga." Albert of Riga or Albert of Livonia (German: Albrecht; c. 1165 - January 17, 1229) was the third Bishop of Riga in Livonia. In 1201 he founded Riga, the modern capital of Latvia, and built the city's cathedral in 1221. Albert headed the armed forces that forcibly converted the eastern Baltic region to Christianity in a crusade that was undertaken while the Fourth Crusade was sacking Constantinople. Albert and his brother Hermann were members of the powerful Buxhoeveden family from Buxtehude, near Loxstedt, Germany. Because of this, he has also been known as Albert of Buxhoeveden (or Bexhövede, Buxhövden, Buxhöwde, Buxthoeven, Appeldern).

Bishop Albert was a canon in Bremen. On March 28, 1199, his uncle, Archbishop Hartwig von Hamburg-Bremen, appointed him Bishop of Livonia (today it is called Latvia and is a part of Estonia) if he could conquer it and convert its inhabitants to Christianity. In the beginning of the year 1200, Albert started the conquest and Christianization of the Baltic's with the support of the German King Philip and the Pope Innocent III. A fleet of twenty-three vessels brought with him carried more than 1,500 crusaders to the Baltic shore.

Together with merchants from the island Gotland, he founded 1201 Riga (today is the capital from Latvia). In 1202, he created the Order of the Sword brothers, and in 1207, King Philip appointed him Prince of the Holy Roman Empire, receiving Livonia as a fief. In 1215, he started building the cathedral of Riga. On November 11, 1225, King Henry VII confirmed for Albert and his brother, Bishop Hermann I von Buxhoeveden, the title of Prince. It took more than twenty-seven years, but Albert accomplished the conquest of Livonia and Estonia and declared his diocese independent from Bremen (Riga became later an archbishopric). In the process, Albert von Buxhoeveden won the admiration of all the political and ecclesiastical powers of his time for this great enterprise (the Pope, the German King and Emperor, the Danish King etc.). He is one of the most important bishops of the thirteenth century, and was venerated as a Saint in Riga, celebrated the first of June. Albert died in Riga in 1229 and left no descendants. The present day 'von Buxhoeven' are descendants of his cousin, Johannes von Buxhoeveden. Albert's brother, Theodoricus, is the forefather of the family de Raupena (de Ropa, known today as 'von der Ropp') that founded manors in Livonia and Courland. A street in Riga, Alberta iela ('Albert Street'), was named after Bishop Albert. The street is known for its Art Nouveau apartment buildings, many of them designed by the architect Mikhail Eisenstein.

Baltic County and a Buxhoeveden's Legacy

I found an article about where my mother's father's side came from, and it tells a great deal about this flourishing and bustling area today. Apparently it has become quite a sheik town and even my cousin, my mother's late brother Theodore's son, had visited the area not too long ago during a business trip. It seems that our family's crest not only held a position of power back then, but also harvested a family-made and owned beverage, Buxhoeveden Vodka! You can imagine our pleasant surprise to this rare find, but it only led us to more disappointment in the family. As wonderful as it was to believe this could be a great find for the family, we had no way of retrieving even just one bottle. Apparently when my cousin went over, he wasn't allowed to bring any home for my mother. You can't even take it out of the country, so unless you wanted to hike your way over, it just wasn't happening. But, it was still nice to know that bit about the family's beverage. Personally, I am not a Vodka drinker, but it's interesting just the same. Without further ado, I'll explain a bit about this incredible region in Baltic County. It's being deemed as a fresh new European destination, looking to Latvia's capital city.

When Latvia joined the European Union, Riga became a favored destination among European travelers looking for a fun weekend-getaway destination. International crowds are also traveling to this place. To clarify Riga is Latvia's capital city and boasts a thriving restaurant scene, vibrant nightlife, and world-class hotels. I seriously doubt this was the way it was back when my grandfather reigned. I am sure he would approve though. The town recently completed a $30 million renovation and expansion at Riga International Airport (RIX). So, the city is poised to reclaim its pre-war nickname, 'The Paris of the Baltic's.'

I think that's very neat and I'm glad to hear it lives on. When battles take place and deaths are left, not only do just the bodies rot but it leaves an impression. This impression is what sometimes leads to haunted grounds, castles, manors, crumbling fortresses etc. So, my take is that if there are any ghosts in Riga from that period, I am sure they're never leaving. With great dining, entertainment, and renovations, it's a good time to be a ghost!

Riga traces its origin to 1201, when Bishop von Buxhoeveden of Bremen founded the first German fort in the Baltic's there as a bridgehead for the crusade against the Northern heathens.

Hence our family book, written in German, titled, Riga 1201 Buxhoeveden 2001 Riga. It looks great inside the book and thank goodness it has pictures! I mean it's in German! But when you see the extended cousins and relatives from the family, it leaves you with a proud heritage-type feeling. There is only so much one could feel when they don't personally know these people, but you do feel something. Catherine will be the next one to take a trip, for the Buxhoeveden Annual Reunion in the fall. They're going to faint when they see her! But, it is long overdue as we are all scattered about the country. It is, simply put, nice to have them around.

Back to the history lesson: Riga quickly grew as a trading point between Russia and the West, and in 1282 joined the Hanseatic League, Europe's powerful trading block. German domination had continued for roughly seven hundred years, and Riga's coat of arms to this day combines the key of Bremen with the towers of Hamburg.

Now, when I was growing up, I had always seen the Buxhoeveden crest in my home. Hans kept it and still has this ancient antique coin dresser. It sits in the entranceway of the Upper West Side apartment. As a child I remember sneaking into the cabinet, slowly opening one panel, to look inside for hidden treasures. The first thing I remember was the odd odor. It wasn't anything pungent, but rather musty and stale from Hans' old coin collection. I remember that Hans would sometimes open up the cabinet and take out a coin or two. Then he'd call me over. "Come here Shoura, I have something to show you," he'd say. (Before

I go any further, I should tell you that my nickname is Shoura, which is short for Shourik and in Russian means Alexander, hence calling me Alexandra.) "Yes daddy," I called back. "Come here please. I'd like to show you this coin," said Hans. So I walked over to the opened, musty smelling cabinet, and looked up at Hans examining this odd coin. It looked like silver, but was very dark and warped. It had some guy on it riding a horse and a lot of twirly-like artwork around it. "Do you know what this is?" asked Hans. As if I always knew, which of course I never did, yet each and every time he insisted on asking that same thing. "No, what is it?" I'd reply. "This, my dear, is a sixth century Byzantine coin, which is very old," explained Hans. He lost me after that, as it always ended up in a history lesson. Now don't get me wrong, I love history, but at the age of eight, I was not very in tune with our world and culture. Kermit the Frog was more my speed, but Hans and I would have our weekly coin talks just the same. I'd nod in agreement and understanding and he would proudly teach me about his latest addition.

Okay, now back to the Baltic's. Like the other Baltic states, Lithuania and Estonia, Latvia was colonized and conquered through the ages by the Poles, the Swedes and the Russians, each leaving evidence of their influence along with a growing distaste among the nationalist Latvians for foreign rule. So, Latvia declared its independence and operated as an independent state between the two world wars. During that era, it was recognized by Western diplomats, journalists, and spies as an ideal center from which to eavesdrop on Stalin's Soviet Union. A predominance of flourishing nightclubs, restaurants and intellectual life earned Riga the nickname 'Little Paris,' but it wasn't until 1991 that Latvia was able to finally declare again, and maintain, its independence.

When I hear that a country was able to reclaim anything, it's a sign of the war left behind and is a bit depressing. So, I'd like to educate you about the positives of Riga today. Riga is a bustling center for the arts. Catherine definitely needs to go there not only as a family member, but as an artist. Redevelopment and innovation seem to be evident everywhere. In May of 2007, Latvia's first female president, Vaira Vike-Freiberga, hosted U.S. President George W. Bush and his wife, Laura, at a series of meetings in Riga where Bush honored Latvia's struggle for independence. This is one of the pictures I was mentioning about being in the Riga Family book. With all the photo opportunities surrounding the event, the world finally caught a glimpse of Riga's visual splendor: the beautiful guildhalls, the astonishingly preserved Old Town, but especially the city's art nouveau, or Jungendstil, architecture, recognized by UNESCO as being the finest in Europe. Crafted in the late nineteenth and early twentieth centuries, the stunning architecture has survived fairly unblemished in Riga — an inadvertent result of the limited availability of funds earmarked for redevelopment during the war-torn twentieth century. My grandfather would be proud. If one would take a walking tour of Riga, you'd get a taste of its past and an inkling of its future. Happily, vehicles are restricted in the city's Old Town, so walkers can proceed unimpeded in an urban center where the drivers are notoriously aggressive (sounds like New York City). It has the Dome Cathedral, home to one of the biggest pipe organs in Europe. Constructed in 1884 by Germany's E.F. Walker & Co., it boasts 6,718 pipes and is laden with wooden carvings dating to the seventeenth and eighteenth centuries. This is history and what I love to absorb. Whether Catherine's family was there or not, all of us came from somewhere and have family trees deeply rooted, all around the world. It is very exciting.

Emails from a distant Buxhoeveden cousin keep us informed about the city and the best of the best. It is suggested to tour early in the day.

By afternoon, street bands offer an undeniable temptation to settle in at one of the many outdoor cafes that line the square and to enjoy the local beer, Aldaris. To me, Aldaris sounds like a far, far away planet. Latvia's national liqueur is Rigas Balzams and is said to be thick and syrupy. Locals love it and swear it's the cure for just about anything that ails you. Legend has it that when Catherine the Great fell ill while visiting Riga, a taste of Balzams allowed her to rise almost magically from her sickbed. I wish we had some of that here back home! Catherine and my uncle, Daniel Buxhoeveden, Count Alexander's last child, would love the culture. If my late Uncle Theodore and late Aunt Rosemarie Buxhoeveden were around, they would as well. Music is everywhere, and you'll hear local violinists, guitarists and opera singers as you continue your stroll. They even have a lift to ancient baroque St. Peter's Church. There is a dazzling 360-degree view of the region. They are gigantic zeppelin hangars brought in from Vainode, a town in western Latvia, in 1924 to house the ancient markets that have existed in Riga since its founding. They provide fourteen acres of space for up to 1,250 sellers, though the spill over into the surrounding streets makes it feel like a lot more. Apparently here is where Hans would love to visit as they have pig heads, obscure cheeses and anything Hans would deem worthy of a sale. This would be an open European flea market for him. Seeing the spectrum would fuel dreams for years to come. Not quite Disneyland, but very nice anyway. Unlike some of us proud New Yorkers, Latvians are by and large honest, and not overly pushy. Even if you don't speak the language (which could be Latvian or Russian or anything in between), pointing and gesturing goes a long way toward making the deal you seek. Here Hans would thrive and I do believe we'd never see him again as he would disappear into the ancient market forever.

Chapter Five:

THE BIG COMMISSION

Catherine started dating Hans when he was producing "The Artist & Models Ball" at the Kit Kat Club in New York City. Catherine and her sister Rosemarie both had to create costumes and some of the outfits they ended up doing were rather riske' for the times. Catherine began attending readings and seances with Hans. It was about this time when Hans had just received the 'Eileen Garret' (monetary) grant from the Paranormal Foundation.

The year was 1962 and Hans was just starting out his life as a new spouse, was soon to be new father, and had lost his parents, and Catherine's brother in a fatal car accident. There was no other family in New York City other than the one he was creating. He would soon create his own circle of friends, which would become the people I grew up with, but for now, Hans was ambitiously writing musical scores in hopes of getting them produced on Broadway or as many off, off Broadway's.

Hans' name and reputation was becoming more known as his interests in the paranormal and with history grew. Hans was a highly educated individual; he had been a student at the University of Vienna and Columbia University and acquired his Ph.D in London, England. He then taught at the New York Institute of Technology for Parapsychology. He created his own company name, Aspera Ad Aspera, Inc., a film production company in New York City for which he always wanted to produce his own projects. The company's name is still imprinted on the inside of his books. For awhile he had his own radio program on station WMCA. And, during all of this, he was about to get a big commission....

Enter Eileen Garret and The Eileen Garret Foundation. She was the president of the only well-known and respected parapsychology foundation at that time. No one really wrote much about ghosts and hauntings, let alone researching them — until Hans came to New York and broke all the rules.

This very famous woman had heard about Hans and was taken by him. She had the power to put him in a position of belonging to something greater. Eileen commissioned Hans to go around the United States and investigate haunted houses and spiritualist camps. His job was to either prove or disprove what the findings were. For two years, Hans traveled extensively with Catherine and his first medium, the great Ethel Johnson Meyers (like the Great Houndini from Snoopy). Catherine assisted with the sound recorder and getting to know the owners of the houses while Hans took the psychic around to get her impressions before starting with the actual investigation of the haunting.

"We did this work (inside) beautiful homes, apartments, in the Village, in Hell's Kitchen, and a townhouse owned by June Havoc," Catherine said. "Outside in the New England country, in Indian territory, by large rocks down south — that's where I met southern hospitality, at cocktail parties given by the local society. Each place had its own character. Hans was well organized in his work. In the states I did the driving while Hans navigated. We basically worked well together because I did what he needed to get done."

The part where my mother says "Hans navigated," I have to stop the press here and make a remark. If you have ever had the privilege of traveling with my father, you'd understand. But being the probability of that is nil to none, I'll give you an idea: Hans, with Catherine in the front driving, is like watching a poorly put on puppet show, where the fingers show through the puppets faces and they knock over the set hence ruining the entire show! Another way to look at it is like two pelicans fighting over a fish. One pelican thinks he's got it while the other insists HE has it. Only one can be right. If the radio was on, it would be too loud for Hans and if the air was on, it would be too cold for Hans. Nothing was ever right for him and unless you wanted to hear complaint after complaint, you'd better get it right the first time. This I believe is how he was able to forge ahead in the ghost business. He just knew what he wanted and knew how it should be. Catherine, making her sighs, silently would thrust the air vents down, turn the radio knob lower, and look out her windshield as the rain began to pour hard. What would come next? Hans would say the wipers are going to fast, slow them down and, that my friends, is one example of what it was like when Hans "navigated."

Story upon story, Hans began a collection of what would become his first book. But he just didn't sit right down and do it. That would be too easy. No, he had to pay his dues and deal with those from beyond and try and get them back to the right place. Not a very glamourous job. The rooms and homes were always cold, maybe an odor would permeate the air, and you're always standing around, waiting for a response. Some ghosts are slow, resulting in what could be a long, drawn out day.

One day Eileen had a talk with Hans. She told him that he needed to write a book. Hans shook his head and told her about his goal of the Broadway musical. So, she sang to him, "write the book." Hans sat down at the desk that still remains in his office as we speak, and began typing away on his Smith Corona. Type, type, type. Henceforth a new birth in the Holzer household! *Ghost Hunter* was published in 1964, and was widely accepted and sought after, that it went into eleven printings. Even by today's standards, that is considered no small potatoes. He had found his true calling — even as the ghosts and spirits were calling on him….

The 1960s was a big time for ghosts. In *Ghost Hunter*, there is a chapter titled "Fifth Avenue Ghost" in which he got the call from Eileen. Hans, Ethel and the group raced across town with their tape recorders and cameras. They were able to identify the ghost as a man from the Civil War who was angered over his death by his girlfriend's other beau.

Yikes! Love is love in any dimension I suppose.

Hans and Ethel helped the ghost lay to rest when they explained to him where he was and that he needed to move on towards the light.

Hans' book opened the doors for so many people from around the world, as they too encountered the strange and unusual. Not like today, where we have so many reality television shows and dozens of ghost hunters and ghost chasers. It's been commercialized and you really don't know what the real deal is anymore. It's more for entertainment purposes rather than value and meaning. Those who really care about the field stand out, and those who don't look silly trying. Now that's spooky to me. Though I will give credit where credit is due, in that some of the mediums on these shows are real and gifted. We have better technology to pick up more sounds than in the old days and we get to see it live all around the world, as well as on our computers as orbs and apparitions go zipping about. But, Hans did pave the way by using the basics to achieve the same bone-chilling realizations that we do after we leave our earthy vessels. Some of us cross over well and some of us don't. The fact is there are restless ghosts in need of help like a wounded animal. There are things that exist beyond our human comprehension and our capabilities to understand our time on earth is limited. We may have to return someday. I'd like to believe we are a society that can take the good with the bad and have beliefs that are constructive, and not destructive. As a result of his efforts, Hans became The Father of Paranormal.

My father has been, and still is, very good at keeping his beliefs and helping those in need. Off on a bit of a tangent I know, but it is crucial in order to understand what kind of a human being Hans is. He wasn't merely just hunting down the distraught dead, but also helping people feel some sort of relief that they weren't going crazy. That they could once again live their lives in their homes in peace. Some hauntings were worse than others, but help was on the way and it didn't come with a cap and booties. Just a regular Nikon and tape recorder with silver, red and blue buttons on it. Hans had pioneered the art and risk-taking of meeting the dead, dead on. Those who were afraid to mention the word did no longer. This is not only what Eileen saw in him, but what propelled him into the unknown.

In 1974, three years after my birth, Hans became the research director for the New York Community Investigation of Paranormal Occurrences. He lectured, wrote, and produced documentaries on psychic subject matters. Not to shabby, eh? From 1976 to 1977, he wrote, produced, and co-hosted "In Search Of" with actor Leonard Nemoy for NBC. Hans was quickly becoming a TV personality and did shows like "In The Thick of the Night" hosted by actor Alan Thicke and "Live With Regis and Kathie Lee." He still wrote music as a composer and lyricist and playwright, and staged musicals. I'm getting out of breath just thinking about all of this. By this point, he had really made a place for himself in the community as a well respected "nut job."

"I also started doing Pen and Ink drawings, illustrating many of the books," recalled Catherine. That resulted in her doing radio interviews and talk shows from California to New York, including the Virginia Graham Show. "I remember standing in the wings (then we wore dresses not pants) and my knees were shaking. I died a thousand deaths before, but did go on to discuss the investigations and my doing the drawings."

My sister and I wouldn't have our first ghostly experiences until the house in Austria. It was exactly like the one featured in the movie, "The Sound of Music," however, we weren't exactly the von Trapps; my mother and aunt were the only ones who could carry a tune, and it wasn't the hills that were alive but rather that darn farm house. The farm house that my mother converted over as a summer place. That will be discussed later on, so hang on to that thought.

Chapter Six:

Party at the Holzer's

I t was New Year's Eve, sometime in the 1970s. Catherine was rushing about getting the food ready, putting all the drinks out and there was always, always a punch bowl at the center table. A clear and red bottomed bumpy patterned style looking bowl. Everything was organized around that darn punch bowl.

I guess back in the 1970s that was the thing to do. My sister, who was eight full years ahead of me, was nowhere to be found. I am not sure if one of us was an "oops," but no matter we were here and that was that. All for a purpose that I now believe in, as to why my sister and I were born.

The apartment walls had red velvet swirl designs and the carpets were also red and oriental patterned. There were tassels hanging from the ceiling with curtains at the doorways with more tassels. *Very odd now that I think about it, but it was normal for that era. I must have been around six years old, so my sister would have been around fourteen.*

My sister Nadine also had a talent in the family business. She could do the most amazing disappearing act anyone has ever witnessed. She'd go so far into her room, that not even the cat – and yes it was a black cat – could find her! She was hiding in her room, watching TV, and gabbing on the phone, while I was stuck out there with the enemy that evening. Oh yes, it was like that year after year. She could escape, but I… I had to hold down the fort until it was all clear. Clear to raid the fridge, clear to go pee, and… just all clear in general. *Now that I think about that, as an adult, she was the smart one!*

So the party was under way and all these weird smelling folks started showing up. Sometimes in pairs, other times, single. The women wore long, seemingly complicated-designed gowns that made you dizzy after awhile if you stared too long at them. Their hair was of great abundance and their skin over perfumed. The apartment on Riverside Drive became a swanky sworay in a matter of minutes. It was show time! Everyone would sit around the coffee table, one of which Catherine rotated every so often with the oblong marvel one.

We were sitting around the wooden circular one this time. Hans had gathered most of the guests like the pied piper, sitting them all nicely as if he were lining all his ducks in a row. It was kindergarten all over again. I'd sit quietly, wondering what was coming next. My sister was free in her room and my mother was entertaining the other guests who hadn't heard my father's call. The couch, the fading armchairs, and some rickety seats supported our fannies as he began his storytelling. This was the part I looked forward to with adoring anticipation. The part that made the whole evening worthwhile. Hans had that knack for storytelling and grabbing your attention right away. And he hadn't even brought out the ghosts yet! That was his parlor trick for the end. Of course the ending is the best part. He began this particular tale about the time he and my mother stayed at a haunted castle in England. Of course this was in one of his books — he took a part of it and went on....

He had been asleep in one of the castle rooms (can you imagine?) when he was visited by a ghost. A man wearing a green pin-striped suit glided a few feet off the floor towards him. He could only be seen from his waist and up, and there was a hat that tipped in front of where his face would be. Hans, sensing his presence, spoke to the entity without lifting an eyelid or raising a brow. He told the ghost to please go away and let him sleep. Could he come back tomorrow? Well, the ghost didn't know what to do, so he just faded back into the wall and disappeared. Later on Hans' stay at the castle, he found out the ghost was not at rest and needed a bit of guidance and a push towards the light.

When I think about this story, I picture now in my mind as a grown up a gangster type of a person. But not from this time, but rather from the 1950s!

My father helped this British ghost by talking to it and recognizing its situation. Apparently that was all that was needed — by Hans acknowledging the ghost's presence and horrible situation, it became quiet during the rest of his stay. However, there is no way of knowing whether or not the ghost left or was satisfied for the time being. One would have to go back and re-investigate the case.

My mother and father traveled quite a bit before I came along. They would go to churches or people's homes when the calls came in about odd "disturbances," like a force greater than them was at work.

I think Star Wars may have existed long before its time. Forces of evil, disturbances in the force, 'may the force be with you,' little green things etc. etc. etc, there's a connection here I just know it! I'll close this chapter with one last story...

There was a seance held at our New York City apartment. Those involved with this seance were Hans, Catherine, Rosine, and Rosine's second late husband's sister. Nadine was very young and was in what would become my room years later. The seance was held in the dining room, which was later made into two rooms by Catherine, to make an extra bedroom for my sister. Hans had a round wooden table in the middle of the room. Everyone placed their hands over the table as not to touch it in anyway. They began inviting a spirit to respond.

"One creek for yes, two for no, and so it went. It started responding then the table started going around the room as we followed it... then we stopped," Catherine recalled. Being that there wasn't a medium on hand, no one could translate what the spirit needed to say so the evening was filled with grown people chasing around a moving table for awhile. *I'm sorry to have missed those days!* Catherine went on to talk about her mother's sister Paulette, the 'other' Parisian in the family. "My Aunt Paulette, your great aunt, was psychic. She would hear things moving down the hall from where we lived in Paris as young girls... so it runs a bit in the family," Catherine said.

I had the distinct pleasure of meeting my great aunt and uncle in Paris on a school trip at age thirteen. They always spoke French and claimed they couldn't speak a word of English. I think they were trying to keep my French up as I was there staying with a French family, where I had to speak the language. I held my own! My great aunt was very graceful and elegant and so was her husband Pierre. He always smoked cigars, drank, and looked like something out of a 1930s film with his swanky hat and tailored coat. They took me out to lunch, and I don't know what we ate, but I remember that green, mint tasting drink! I believe I was also offered a cigarette, but turned it down. Of course, smoking out there was normal and very well accepted. Hans would have had a heart attack if he knew. Sadly, only a few months after my visit with these incredible people, both Paulette and Pierre passed within a short time of one another. They were true lovebirds and when one went, the other wounded bird was not far behind.

Chapter Seven:

The Holidays

How does one celebrate what has come to be known as 'Turkey Day' in a vegan home? Answer: very carefully and bring your sense of humor. The battles between Catherine and Hans, with my sister and I in the middle, were about to begin. Thank goodness Rosine was there to take off some of the culinary pressure. We all loved our Nana. She made everything okay, and in her heavy french accent, calmed the beast. Catherine sometimes would make turkey, but also enjoyed cooking a Virginia ham with pineapples and cherries. Hans felt like he was on the attack — that my mother was doing that on purpose and how dreadful it was to smell that foul beast in his kitchen. It was too hilarious for words. My sister and I just looked on, trying to bottle up our bursting laughter at the seams. I just couldn't resist and had to let it all out. First came the look from Catherine to quiet down. Next, Nana was pointing her finger at me up and down. But the best was yet to come — Hans' reaction to all of it. Catherine would take out the ham or turkey depending on the year and begin to carve it. Hans announces that he will only enter the kitchen when the beast has left. I call out that the coast is all clear sarcastically, as Nana gives me a whack across my head. It was funny... I didn't care how many times I got reprimanded. Hans was insane about meat being cooked in that house. This I am sure drove a partial annoying wedge between him and Catherine. *Later on you will read in one of Hans and Catherine's newspaper interviews, the beginning tension about food in the Holzer household.* The meat was put out regardless and, to Hans' chagrin, his children enjoyed it very much.

Hans never pushed his vegetarian philosophies on us when we were young oddly enough. But, he did lecture out loud, trying to get his point across. It wouldn't be until later on in life that he began to lecture more to my sister and I about what meat does to the body and why you shouldn't eat eggs.

I remember explaining as a teenager to my friends about the food pyramid in my house. It wasn't that lovely and colorful chart you see on the packages of bread or backs of cereal boxes. No, not in Hans' house. It was a circle filled with vegetables, tofu and soy. Suffice to say, my friends and I ate out most of the time. I made the mistake once of inviting a very popular girl to my house in the hopes I would get into her "click." I set up the dinner table and we had candles and music. Hans offered to make the dinner and I felt at the time that he'd know to at least make spaghetti and rolls — a meal most children can eat. My friend and I sat down at our table awaiting Hans' lovely meal. Since she was enthralled with his books and life, we had much to discuss. Then it happened — the mistake I mentioned a few sentences back. In walks Hans with a large tray of food. Do you think there was anything digestible on it? That was the original plan, but to my horror and embarrassment, the opposite occurred. Mounds of brussel sprouts next to humus in a bowl, wheat bread piled up to the ceiling, and an enormous bowl of salad overflowing and dropping onto the carpet. My friend looked at me as if she'd seen a ghost. Now, on any other given circumstance that would make sense, but not that evening. I hadn't the heart to be rude as I was brought up with manners, so I thanked him and then explained the Holzer food circle in hopes this girl would forgive the odd evening. Thankfully, I made her laugh and we tossed brussel sprouts at one another while using the over-toasted bread as ping pong paddles. I did well in that game too. That was the beginning and end to dinners at home with friends.

Many families do sit down to dinner at the same time each evening. In the Holzer house, that wasn't quite the way. My sister would rush to eat or would have already eaten, and I usually was stuck in the middle, being much younger. I had less power than she. There I was in our galley-style kitchen, night after night staring at my plate of food. The phone would ring and a chance for me to make a break for it became possible. Catherine would get up from the table to answer it while Hans sat there yelling out, "Who is it? Tell them it's dinnertime and I'll call them back whoever it is!", he grunted as he went back to chewing his salad. A salad that he never missed at dinnertime. He loves salad so much that he would have it for lunch as well. To fully appreciate a salad made by Hans, one must understand his expertise in vegetables and grocery shopping. The type of salad Hans would buy would come with a rubber band around it. You know the kind I mean, the salad that was just uprooted from it's earthy home? In any case, first he had to wash the salad. Now most of us use colanders to wash and drain our foods. Not Hans. We had a double sink because we never had a dishwasher put in. So, it was all sink. One side he had some dirty dishes in, and the other he plugged up and filled with water. Then he did the unthinkable to that poor salad. He throws it in the filled up sink and lets it sit there for awhile. Then, he'd come back to it and pull it out and get a huge salad bowl. Then came the scissors. Now this always confused me as I could hear him cutting in the kitchen the same time each day. So, curious, I peered in one afternoon and saw him attack the salad! Over the big bowl, he was cutting the salad into chunks without removing that rubber band. When it came time for dinner, Hans took my bowl and placed salad in it. First he'd get his concoction of homemade salad dressing. This is where Rosine was really needed for a visit. Her salad dressing was intoxicating in every way. My sister and I would beg her to make extra before she'd go back home, so that we could survive another week of Hans' homemade batch.

Hans didn't like purchasing supermarket brands, as he felt they were filled with all sorts of evils. On this particular evening, we were out of luck. Hans proceeded to pour his version of Nana's dressing over my bowl, drowning each chunk of salad. What was I going to do? Catherine sat back down at the table as we were suppose to begin eating. I was afraid of my food! If you had witnessed the attack that I had earlier in the day, you'd understand. But I was still obligated to try the salad anyway. The first bite wasn't so bad, but when I went for the second, there it was staring back at me. A piece of pink rubber band flip flopping in between my fork groves. The phone rang again. It did that a lot in the Holzer house. Actually, it probably rang somewhere in the neighborhood of twenty plus times a day and then there was night. Nighttime was a whole different breed of calls in our home. I'd estimate somewhere around an added thirty calls. This time Hans got up from the table as he detested being disturbed around dinnertime. He answered the phone abruptly and quickly hung up the receiver. Not enough time for me to escape, I am afraid to say. Being we were cat people at the time, I couldn't feed anything under the table so I was running out of options. The fact that our kitchen was long and thin gave me a short distance between the table and the garbage can. Hans and Catherine were conversing, so I took the opportunity at hand.

Quickly pulling my bowl towards me, using the cloth underneath, I was able to maneuver the drop off. I spun to the side of the garbage can and pretended to sneeze. In the process, I tossed the salad and turned back around, replacing the bowl where it originally was. Hans and Catherine blessed me and went on with their conversation. I had succeeded and it was a triumphant moment! There after, I was able to eat the rest of my dinner and be excused without anyone knowing the better.

Hans had his ways of doing things from cooking, shopping and dressing to anything else in between. That's who he was and still is — a brilliant mind with anal and neurotic tendencies. It's an explosive mix, but his heart is of gold and more than makes up for it. One would have to be smart growing up in this family and very patient. I was doomed from the start.

Christmas was also an interesting time. There was the buying of the tree. It wouldn't go without saying if Hans didn't argue that as well. His whole theory on cutting down the poor defenseless pine trees poured over us like syrup to a pancake, smothered and stuck. He'd say it wasn't very nice to place it in our home watching it die for two weeks. This was regurgitated each season. In Hans' mind that was cruelty to the tree. He may have been correct, but as a child, not to have a tree would have been a sin. The tree was the best part and, as loving as he was, he went along with that too. Catherine would get a plan of action together as she rounded up Hans, Nadine and I for the tree buying ceremony. Keep in mind this was in New York City where you lugged what you bought. We paraded up and down Broadway, looking at each tree. They were lined up as if newly assassinated and waiting to be dragged off for the rest of their impending doom. The doom of the decorating ceremony with sharp hooks and burning lights. This is how Hans saw it. Catherine would walk up to the owner of these lovely trees and start pulling them one by one checking out their height and fullness. Through Catherine, I realized there was a real art form in selecting the perfect tree. I began at that very moment around age eight to appreciate the holiday spirit. The excitement just took off from there. *I haven't changed a bit since then and still act like that eight year old when buying a tree for my own children.* Catherine then turned to Nadine and I and asked what we thought. Together we chose what seemed at the time the perfect tree. For an extra few dollars, they trimmed the sappy stump and tied her up to go. Notice I gave a gender to the tree. Everything was a she when I was a child. So, the tree became like a temporary family member, and it was going home with me that night. Hans muttered under his breath as Catherine yelled at him to "grab the stump, grab the stump!" Hans, being the unnatural athlete that he was, dropped the stump more then ten times on the way back home. I almost peed myself as my sister tried once again to contain her laughter. Catherine was losing it and Hans never had it. Finally, we reached our destination back at the building.

Catherine commanded our little army forward into the building's side door, hauling this tree to the elevator. Of course when the elevator doors opened, Catherine began to angle out the tree while Nadine and I became buried under it's pines. Hans was shoved into the corner as Catherine held most of the tree. No one could reach the buttons to push floor eight. "Well, someone push the damn button!" belted out an annoyed Catherine. Frantically, Hans would look for the button but not without yelling back at Catherine, "All right, all right, give me a second! I can hardly move." That did it. I bursted out laughing and Nadine was sure to follow. I could hear my mother's eyelids roll. When the elevator door opened, Nadine and I stumbled out with pines and sap all over us, and crawling to our front door in agony because we had to use the bathroom. Hans, panicking because he is claustrophobic, nearly ran Catherine and the tree down to get out of his boxed corner. Finally everyone was inside and Catherine lay the tree up against a huge wall mirror in the living room. There it would sit as she devised the second part of the plan. At this point, Catherine ordered Hans out of the room, and much to his delight, left. The remaining hours would consist of Catherine, Nadine and I, and the cat to decorate our tree. When it was all over, Hans was allowed back into the living room as he then could fully enjoy the ritual of buying the tree. After all was said and done, he did like it and was happy to see his family enjoying it as well. But, not without strife or chaos did these rituals come with.

As for the gift giving, the one thing that I feel to share is this. Each year the night before Christmas some families open their gifts on Christmas Eve. Growing up, we opened our gifts Christmas Day or also called Christmas morning. Out of everyone in the house, I was the most impatient one of all. I disliked the fact that we had to wait to open our gifts while others could do so one day ahead. I would question why couldn't we open ours on Christmas Eve? Catherine would explain that Christmas Eve is when we host and only exchange with the adults. Santa's gifts were to be dropped off while we were asleep. I can see now that she was trying to keep with tradition of the tale of, *The Night Before Christmas*, but it still stunk! Hans, seeing my difficulty with this ritual, began to feel bad for me. He started his own gift giving with me. Of course my sister could partake, but I don't recall her being into this new idea as much as I was. Mainly due to the fact we were so far apart in age during the early years. Unbeknownst to Catherine, Hans pulled me aside and explained to me his plan of action. From now on for Christmas Eve, after all the guests went home, he would give me one gift to open. This was the greatest moment of my Christmas life. I lived for that ritual. Catherine never knew until later on, in which case she didn't mind. Perhaps at the time Hans felt she would have frowned upon as there was tradition and to keep with it. Hans' softer side caved into my big blue eyes and it was a father/daughter moment.

Chapter Eight:

The Witches' Ball

My school friends' parents went to their holiday office parties in suits, and they were held at fancy restaurants or at the office itself. Hans went to The Witches Ball for his office party and so the normalcy of it all, flew right out the window along with Jacob Marley and his crew of Christmas ghosts from the Past, Present and Future. Every Hallows Eve, Hans would get all dolled up for The Witches Ball. The aroma in the air would change from stale coffee to an aqua velva type cologne. The clanking of chains and rustling of belts could be heard from my room. Hans was frantically getting dressed for this prestigious event. An event that was filled with stars in the outer realms of earth. You wouldn't see the George Clooneys or Brad Pitts at these events, no you would see the 'other' stars. The individuals who claimed to read the stars and planetary alignments, individuals who came with an extra deck of tarot cards, and individuals with oversized rings that could tell the future.

I always wondered what it was like inside one of those events; growing up, I imagined long tables enveloped with red crushed velvet cloths and crystal balls as center pieces.

An "ah, here it is" and another "one second, one second" and then it was done. Hans was satisfied with his chosen ensemble of which Catherine had nothing to do with. This was not a good thing as she was well coordinated.

For example, at my wedding, where all the men wore black tux's, Hans insisted on wearing his blue tux from ancient times. Oh, his bow tie was black, so he deemed that good enough.

Then the announcement came from the center of the living room. "I'm leaving!" Hans would shout. Since no one responded, I felt the need to fill that spot. "Okay, have fun storming the castle!" *Actually I didn't say that as some of you may recognize that line from the film "Princess Bride."* However, I did yell back and came out of my room to give him a hug and kiss. There Hans was with his black, wide collard, opened button down shirt, and several mystical heavy chains surrounding his hairy neck. His pants were black velvet and swallowed up his shoes. He looked like something out out *Saturday Night Fever*. Add a cape and some white powder make up and you'd have Grandpa Al Louis from the TV show *The Munsters*. In any case, that was Hans and what one could expect him to look like for this auspicious occasion. As he leaned down to kiss my head, one of his large eyeball rings smacked me on the right. Hans made sure that I knew, for the hundredth time, dinner was out and that he wouldn't be back till after midnight. When questioned why so late, he responded, "Why so early? It only gets going at midnight, my love!" With that Hans turned away, grabbing his black, Inspector Clouseau-style raincoat and placed his Hollywood style hat on his greying head. He swung the door open and turned back to say one last thing. "Make sure you lock up after me!" and then he vanished into the abyss of New York City night life and I would be left dreaming what he was doing and who he was meeting. I'd have to wait until daylight to catch a tale or two from him to satisfy my burning need to know.

After a night of dreaming of witches, warlocks, wizards, and magical spells, I ran into the kitchen following the scent of Hans' coffee. One mustn't disturb the great master before he has had his first cup of caffeine. "So?" I asked Hans. "So what?" he replied while cutting up his grapefruit. Frustrated I shouted at him, "Come on, spill the beans. How was last night? What did you do? Who was there?" Hans laughed his deep, honking laugh and delightfully turned my way to respond. *I think now looking back, he was pleasantly surprised I was taking an interest in his social outings and what he enjoyed doing.* "My darling Alex, I will tell you this. It was a wonderful mix of interesting people from all around the world exchanging information. Now, what do you want for breakfast!" I sat there not so much disappointed as I was feeling that perhaps I made too much of this ball. If he had told me the truth, I believe, it may have made him an irresponsible parent at the time. Those balls' had very interesting people yes, however; many delved into the paranormal from one extreme to another. It turns out that the characters at these balls had to be someone in the community of the paranormal and were invited guests. Some were with grand credentials while others a bit off, if you know what I mean.

Hans was considered a warlock, which is a male witch. He had this necklace with a star emblem in a circle. Noticing my fascination with his jewelry, he started to pick some up for me as well. Then I became fascinated with crosses, but not their meaning. For the time being, I began wearing dangling cross earrings and large cross necklaces. Hans would even get some exotic looking ones where, if you didn't know where they came from, you'd think it was an artifact. *It wouldn't be until my adult life that when handed an original family heirloom, I would appreciate its meaning.*

However, this was part of Hans' right of passage in working in the paranormal field. It really did make sense for him to attend such gatherings. In the beginning of Hans and Catherine's marriage,

Catherine attended many events with Hans as she was drawn to their magical and mystical ways. However, after time Catherine pulled back and began to change as an individual and branched out more with her skills in the interior design world. But, she always supported Hans as she understood his passion and complexities in the strange and unknown parallel universe that perhaps sent Hans to her in the first place. Year after year every Halloween, Hans would go through his nightly ritual of getting ready for the witches ball until the wee hours of the morning. *It reminds me of the slogan we hear today, 'what happens in vegas, stays in vegas.' I feel the same about this ball. Some things are better left at the door.*

Chapter Nine:

HAUNTED SUMMER FARM HOUSE

Catherine had agreed to convert a farm house in Austria so my family could enjoy summers among the hills, mountains, and a town that my parents felt very comfortable in. Hans and Catherine purchased a wine-colored Citroen car that I absolutely adored. Hans never drove or even cared to learn how. He was quite content to be driven and Catherine was quite content in doing so. For years, our family was fortunate enough to travel to Europe and see the sights and sounds. During the early 1970s my Parisian grandmother traveled with us. I began my journey to Europe in my lovely, spacious, one-room bassinet. It wouldn't be until I was around one and a half years old that I would learn to walk in those beautiful mountainesque viewed fields. But when we arrived there for our first summer, the "Lady" of the house was expecting us.

Badase, Austria would get immense thunderstorms. I remember Hans and Catherine running about the house pulling all the windows closed as fast as possible. I was around three when I began remembering the way the house would smell and feel to me. In particular, I recall an area rug in the den that my father detested, but came with the house. Catherine liked it of course. It was one of those bear rugs with the actual head and paws spread out like roadkill. I used to like to roll around on it and talk to the head. When I was old enough to tell stories to, Hans told me of a time in this house. I was in my highchair, which at that time had no buckle belts or protection of any kind. It was made in Austria with little hearts cut out of its back. I am sure a beautiful piece of furniture, but not very safe. The five of us were all at the breakfast table as the sun was warmly shining in, when all of a sudden my highchair started to fall backwards. I was moving around too hard in it and my mother was at my side, but couldn't reach me quick enough. The way the chair was falling would have positioned me going backwards onto the hard tiled floor and to an uncertain outcome....

Instead my family witnessed my little body being pulled up in the air and held there in place. Catherine quickly grabbed my legs and middle and pulled me down onto her. That was a breakfast to remember I suppose. Along with the creaking noises we all heard at night, were the sounds of footsteps walking up and down the corridors. At night, Hans, affectionately known as 'The Midnight Raider,' always hit the fridge at midnight for a snack and then went back to bed. Catherine and her mother Rosine stayed put for the most part. They were the types of people that got what they needed before bed so that they could rest. As for my sister and I, we were in the open spaced attic. I remember how it smelled. The pine was so strong and robust. However, ask my sibling and she'll give you a different version of that whole house. Being older and more in tune to things, she had the creeps staying there. Even with Hans as the "Ghost Hunter," would not make a difference to a ten year old.

One night Nadine decided to get out of bed and go downstairs for a drink. *Now my eldest is eight and so they can do that. For my younger ones we have the gate up so that they cannot do that.* I always slept through the night and had a bottle by my side. *Nowadays, that is not good either as bottles should be put away.* Anyway, Nadine proceeded down the stairs towards the kitchen. As she was going back up the stairs, there at the top of the landing stood what appeared to be my grandmother. Back then Rosine would wear these long robes that covered her feet. So it was only natural and normal to assume it was her. Relieved, Nadine went back up the stairs and tugged on Rosine's robe to say come on, let's go back to bed. Only it wasn't Rosine's robe she was tugging on. It was a ghost of a woman who once lived in that house. Looking up to a different face, Nadine ran through the ghost and right back to bed where she draped the covers over her head until morning light.

Every night thereafter she would sleep that way and never went down the stairs alone again. The ghost was the same ghost who saved my life that morning. She was looking after us and shared her home with us. She passed in her seventies and remained there as she chose not to cross over. I believe Hans tried to help her, but she politely refused. Even as a ghost, there are still choices to be made. And so we left the farm house and 'the lady' of that house each summer to return back to New York. Sometimes I wondered if she would follow us, but I believe she sensed my sister's fear and stayed put.

Chapter Ten:

CHARACTERS
NEed NoT Apply

(Tina Louise, Turhan Bey, Yolana Bard, Ethel Johnson Meyers and Sybil Leek...)

G inger Grant... Many men, including my spouse, would whisper her name like a breath of fresh air. She probably helped most young men get through puberty. However, for Hans and myself, she was a family friend and always a joy to have over for some herbal tea and a hearty salad.

When I was around twelve or so, Tina (Louise) was in New York, back and forth with her only daughter. She and I quickly became friends and would hang out at each other's apartments. They were in the lower 70s on Riverside Drive and we were ten blocks up so it worked out well. Sometimes we'd switch our outfits and pretend to be each other. Other times we sat there and sang popular songs of that time. But, my favorite part would be when Tina would come by and have lunch and just be there. Being our kitchen was galley style, the table was small and narrow. I'd sit at one end while she stood on the other side leaning up against the counter. Sometimes the warmth of her smile and smooth tone made me feel like she was another mom in the room. The clanking of her stirring the cup of tea would initiate our conversation. At that time to me, she was one of my father's good friends as he had many. And they too would visit and just go in and out of our fridge helping themselves. My father was very decent that way. His home was their home, and while my mother left my father when I was thirteen, didn't mind at all because it was a nice thing to do and a nice way to be. It had always been that way living with him and was the way they also hosted their parties. It was nice having Tina, among many others, come by and share a story or two over some lunch. When her daughter came, it was fun and I looked forward to seeing her and playing actress.

One time I remember there was a death from the cast of "Gilligan's Island." The Skipper had passed, Mr. Alan Hale Jr., and Tina's daughter had to leave early to go to the funeral. I was sad and wanted to go with her and also pay my respects, but I wasn't allowed. She didn't seem to want to go either. At our age that's not what one called fun, but she reluctantly went and so did my play date for that afternoon.

The one thing I miss about the daughter, was her black and white polka dotted outfit that she lent me. When she had to go, so did that outfit and that was the only thing I had left to remember her with. Time would pass and we would no longer keep in touch. It wouldn't be for over twenty years before I'd have enough courage and reason to call Ms. Louise herself and say "hello." My father always kept up contact with her and she returned the calls. But so much time had passed — I was living my life and so was her daughter. Sometimes in life you need to get to a point where you say the hell with it and, as Arnold Schwarzenegger says, "just doo ittt!" We reconnected and I am so glad because she is a lovely soul to know.

Turhan Bey was a famous English Hollywood actor of the 1940s. He is half Austrian and half Turkish on the father's side. He left Hollywood and became a photographer living near Vienna. "We visited him often and he took great photos of Hans and I, which I still keep in the family album. On one of our trips to Ireland we were hosted by the Bear Guiness Family, if I recall correctly, and had dinner at their Castle outside of the Dublin area. In Scotland I wore my kilt and danced with some Scottish men in theirs! Also spent nice evenings in Scottish homes as well as with an American woman named Elizabeth, living in Scotland who wrote the book on Mary, Queen of Scots," said Catherine. "She was quite the character and visited us when we hosted dinners in our New York apartment. As a result, I did a painting of Hermitage Castle, where Mary, Queen of Scots was imprisoned. It was later photographed in the color section of *The Daily News* and was sold to a reader who saw it."

Yolana Bard, known as "the queen of psychics," began at a young age developing her paranormal intuition. Hans met her before it all exploded into what has become her famed career. She helped celebrities, statesmen, and law enforcement officials, inspiring clients everywhere. She became well known and established a practice and reputation as a good medium. Clients would seek her out from around the world and she tried to help them in any way she could. It was a lot of stress and pressure placed upon her soul, as those who sought her out took up most of her energy. But she truly believed in helping people with her ability to hear those on the other side and pass along messages and answer questions. Yolana was not always this blessed and was at one point without a home. Having her children early eventually became her enemy and anchor at the same time, creating her own belief system to help her through the rough times. Hans stood by her and even wrote about her in his book titled *Physic Yellow Pages*.

Yolana Bard was a close friend of the Holzer family and I remember her name ringing throughout our house from time to time. I was too young to appreciate her, and when I heard of her recent passing, felt horrible. But I knew to accept it and Hans, on the other end of the phone, was saddened and quiet. For the first time in a long time, Hans was quiet. Yolana was a gift who shared her gift and turned it into a business to help others. She had to survive as we all must do. She lived and died doing what she was born to do.

Yolana will be sorely missed among the physic and spiritual community. As one of the world's most highly esteemed psychic mediums, Yolana was regularly consulted on high-profile criminal cases, where she helped numerous police departments solve cases, particularly cases involving missing children. In addition, her private client list included major corporate executives, world leaders, and Hollywood's top celebrities. She at one time was named "New York's Best Psychic." Yolana passed away at home at sixty-six years of age. Hans had great admiration and respect for her as she struggled in her life at such a young age. Hans understood the perils of struggling as he too had traveled that path. Her children, later that week, went over to Hans' for a private moment.

After medium Ethel Johnson Meyers passed, then Medium Sybil Leek, Yolana was the remaining few of Hans' circle of 'special' friends. However, he took solace in knowing the place to where his friends would cross over to and always told them they'd meet up one day. The running joke for Hans of course was that he'd never make it there as St. Peter would tell him to go back. When questioned why, Hans replied that Heaven was in fear he'd take over and Hell didn't want him, so he was left roaming the earth until allowed to enter the kingdom. Hans certainly has a bizarre way of explaining his own time, but that is one of the many qualities that make Hans simply Hans.

Here is a snippet from *Merlian News* on Yolana's passing. "In a world of critics and skeptics, Yolana was known for her exceedingly precise readings. In fact, world-renowned parapsychologist and author Hans Holzer claimed that 'no one can match her track record.' Holzer says that 'a good medium is on target about half the time, while Yolana consistently averaged in the eighty percent range and regularly approached one hundred percent.' For over twenty-five years, Yolana used her abilities to inspire her clients to trust their instincts and look within themselves for the answers they seek. After, they would have 'just one more question.' Those circumstances prompted Yolana to write her autobiography, *Just One More Question*, last year in which she offered readers direction and insight in hope that they would learn to trust their own intuition and attain their own destinies.

"Fifty percent accuracy with a psychic is a desirable state. Yolana has, incredibly enough, been accurate to one hundred percent...I believe she's one of the great psychics of this century."

—*Hans Holzer Ph.D*

"There are few people I have met who can ignite the imagination as she does. Inside her diminutive frame is the power of the universe, proof of the divine. I believe she is an instrument of God's love and guidance."

—Kelsey Grammer,
Television and film actor/
executive producer

There was also an extraordinary woman by the name of Sybil Leek. Below, please find a snippet from the Occultism & Parapsychology Encyclopedia reference section.

Sybil Leek (1922-1982), astrologer, witch, author, and one of the more popular figures in the modern occult revival. She was born on February 22, 1922, in the Midlands, England, and claimed an ancestry in witchcraft through both sides of her family. Through her mother the lineage could be traced to southern Ireland in the twelfth century and through her father to Russia. She was tutored at home and attended school for only four years (ages 12-16). She claimed that she had been initiated into the craft while near Nice, in southern France, and that her initiation was to fill an opening left by the death of her aunt, who had been high priestess of a coven. She then returned to England and settled near New Forest, where she reportedly joined the Horsa Coven, which she claimed predated the Norman Conquest. She soon became high priestess of the group. There is no substantiation of that story and some evidence that it is fabricated. In the early 1950s she claimed to have had a mystical experience in which she realized that her calling in life would be as a spokesperson for witchcraft, the old religion. Her early efforts resulted in tourists flocking to her antique shop, not to buy but to get her autograph. She had a conflict with her landlord, who demanded she renounce her religion, and she eventually had to close her shop. Meanwhile, she had written several books, but none of them dealt with witchcraft. In the early 1960s Leek moved to the United States. With the assistance of her publisher and a set of public relations people, she soon became famous as a public witch. She lectured widely, appeared on television, and built a large clientele as an astrologer. Quietly, she founded, and for a period, led several covens; two in Massachusetts, one in Cincinnati, and one in St. Louis. Leek wrote over sixty books among which were an autobiography, *Diary of a Witch* (1968), and several on witchcraft, including *The Complete Art of Witchcraft* (1971). The material in these books is conflicting. While claiming traditional witchcraft roots, prior to the neo-pagan revival of witchcraft by Gerald Gardner, her own presentation of witchcraft is completely Gardnerian. She talks of ritual items such as the athame (the ritual dagger) as if she had known about them before Gardner. However, we now know that they were invented by Gardner. She seems to have reproduced a variation on Gardner's ritual. It appears as if she, like many in the early decades of the Wiccan revival, created a magical lineage for herself, but in fact obtained her training and knowledge of the craft from Gardnerians. She died in Melbourne, Florida, in 1982.

As one of the few authors Hans could relate to with having the gift of sight, these two were inseparable when the call came to investigate paranormal activity. Sybil and Hans were a great team, and when she passed, I was only eleven years old. But, I felt the sadness fill the Holzer household. As this was two years before Hans and Catherine split up, Catherine was still there to help Hans cope with his loss.

The one thing Hans could always do was handle his emotions with the afterlife and his line of work. He was able to rationalize and concur the moment and move on. With his personal emotions, and especially about his relationship to Catherine, that was very messy and had a sadness of its own. I don't think Hans has fully recovered from his failed marriage even in this day and age. He has simply learned to adapt and move on as so many others have to do.

All these great mediums were sorely missed and Hans and I truly believe they were sent back to a place where they could become strong guardians of others and perhaps one day fulfill another role. Until then, their memories, accomplishments, and marks on this world will remain untouched forever.

Chapter Eleven:

Partying with the...
Psychics, Warlocks, and the Witches of Riverside Drive

*J*ust once I had hoped and prayed that one of my father's friends would come over with a handsome prince. Understand that back then, that was top of my list. But, alas the ones who had sons were too old for me. Back then three years older was like ancient, you know? Or, they just didn't fit that prince charming type. Well, on with the party...

An evening with friends, family, and the movie projector sets up this next scene at the Holzers. The best way I could describe Hans in this type of setting is to compare him to the character played by actor Darren McGavin, the father in the classic and favored holiday movie *A Christmas Story*. Darren also met Hans and Catherine and they got along very well. Catherine adored him and said he was very funny. All the guests would be lined up in the living room on the couch, arm chairs and rowed up on the floor in front of the huge stark white movie screen that I had the distinct honor of pulling down for the waiting audience. One of my many daunting tasks for the evening. Oh joy. The screen was ready and the lights were off except in the entranceway where Hans and the projector stood. He'd be fussing around with large movie reels, as the top reel was placed and then the bottom. It began. Hans became that *Christmas Story* father and for the rest of the evening, created quite an atmosphere for the need to have many, many drinks! As the bottom reel hooked on, Hans turned on the machine and the light hit the middle of the movie screen. Before the numbers could count down, before the little annoying beeping sounds could be heard, something went wrong. A piece of reel came flying out from underneath the second reel as it flickered and flackered against the table it stood on. Everyone stared at the blank screen, then looked back at one very annoyed Hans, then back again at the screen. "Don't anybody mooove!" Hans shouted out. "A reel is out!" On went the lights and everyone took a breath and talked amongst themselves and some lit up their cigarettes and moved their toukus's around to get comfortable once again. I knew what this was the beginning of, but the guests weren't quite sure yet.

I can't help but laugh now as I think back on those times. I mean really, he was so hilariously serious that it made it even harder to control my deep belly laughter that fueled the fire towards my sister. Hans despised that and my revenge on her disappearing acts with company, arrived this very moment. I had waited all year long for this time where now she would feel the wrath of a Holzer function. She'd get blamed for the noise. She'd get blamed for all of it!

As my father fumbled around with the projector, I began to laugh and start imitating Hans. Nadine desperately tried to keep it in, but within seconds started laughing out loud. The guests looked our way. Some looked at us as if we had two heads. Actually we did. Our two heads were bobbling back and forth in hysteria. When Hans caught wind of it, that made it worse and better at the same time. His anger was exactly what I needed for more material to keep the show running. "SILENCE down there, Nadine!" Hans would shout out as he was holding a reel in his hands. He'd shake the reel out at us, but wasn't quite sure where we were as the projector light was so blinding. It would have been nice if he actually turned it off, but he was too involved with fixing the reel. In the midst of all this, you could hear defamatory words being uttered under his frustrated breath. Things like "Dag nab it" and "One second...one second," which I would repeat back to my sister. This continued the roar, which then brought back Hans' attention to her. He didn't care who was in the room as long as he fixed that damn projector. It was his goal, his mission and drive come hell or high water, to show all of us those stupid but scenic Austrian homemade movies where I'm bare naked.

Nice dad, real nice! Nadine was eight years old and I, an infant with no rights or the ability to say "hey some clothes here would be nice, don't' ya think?"

By this time the guests were getting up to go to the bathroom, empty ash trays and go find a drink. Soon, the dining room and kitchen were filled with everyone drinking and smoking and chatter got on its way. Some would speak of the latest greatest film out while others spoke of their favorite actor/actress. "Everyone's a critic," I thought to myself.

The psychics, witches, and warlocks were many of the guests at these gatherings, as they were also authors, actors, singers and believers in their cult and practices. Hans often mixed his gatherings with these personalities and family. Oftentimes, they would provide "readings," as they waited for the show to begin, and smoke filled the air, creating little halo rings. This was the moment I had been waiting for all evening. The finale before the show even began. This was when it was the best. "Come everyone now into the living room! I have fixed it and the movie is beginning. Hurry, hurry!" Hans belted out. Excited, as he once again triumphed over that damn movie projector that was older than dirt! As the herd migrated back to their seats, my sister and I settled down after we had to change our undies twice from laughing so hard. The lights went off again and the sound of the projector started to the countdown from ten to two showing on screen number one. Then as the guests' drinks stirred in their hands, smoke pushing out into the opening of the room, we were in for the long haul. Hans began his evening with his typical comment that always went along with the opening credits to this feature. "Ah the innocent years," as my bare ass was plastered all over the opening scene! But hey, the mountains and boat rides looked great!

Chapter Twelve:

The 'Psychic' Method

Hans sometimes would go beyond storytelling, relying on contacts with the spirits. For a bit of a quick ghostly history lesson, it's important to mention how skeptism played a big role that Hans has had to tackle for over six decades. Thank goodness he doesn't care and keeps his sense of humor! And I quote *Investigative Files for Ghost Hunters* by Joe Nickell, "Belief in such contact is called spiritualism, and it is as ancient as the Old Testament's Witch of Endor who purportedly conjured up the ghost of Samuel at the request of King Saul (I Sam. 28:7 20). Modern spiritualism began in 1848 at Hydesville, New York, when two young girls, Maggie and Katie Fox, pretended to communicate with the ghost of a murdered peddler. Although four decades later they confessed how their 'spirit rappings' had been faked, in the meantime spiritualism had spread across the United States and beyond. Interest in spiritualism inspired ghost hunting. The first organization devoted to the cause was a ghost society formed at Cambridge University in 1851. It was followed by London's Ghost Club in 1862, the Society for Psychical Research (SPR) in 1882 and an American counterpart (ASPR) in 1885. Such organizations attracted both scientists and spiritualists, many hoping to unite science and religion by validating spiritualist phenomena (Guiley 200, 6, 7, 151, 153, 353, 354). Out of that tradition comes Holzer, who terms himself a parapsychologist. In his book *America's Haunted Houses,* he relates his 'investigation' of Ringwood Manor in northern New Jersey. Holzer arrived at Ringwood with 'psychic' Ethel Meyers in tow, a dubious choice given her involvement in the Amityville Horror case wherein she failed to realize it was a hoax. She supposedly made contact with former servants of Ringwood, saying that one, 'Jeremiah,' had 'complained bitterly about his mistress,' a Mrs. Erskine. However, the curator of Ringwood told me he doubted the house was haunted, and disparaged the notion that Mrs. Erskine mistreated any servant whether 'Jeremiah' or not.

"He observed that the present house was never seen by her, and 'isn't even near the location of the original house!' (Prol, 1993) Thus when Holzer writes, 'The center of the hauntings seems to be what was once the area of Mrs. Erskine's bedroom' (Holzer, 1991), he betrays an utter lack of historical credibility. Holzer, while a prolific mystery monger, is not the worst such offender. He observes: 'Amateur investigators can do more damage than good at times, especially when they travel as 'demonologists' looking for demons and devils as the cause of a haunting' (Holzer, 1991). He could be referring to an elderly couple, Ed and Lorraine Warren, who operate something they call the New England Society for Psychic Research. Ed, the director, has a business card that bills him as a 'Demonologist.' Lorraine, sporting a bouffant hairdo, claims to be a 'clairvoyant.' They have been called other things, ranging from 'passionate and religious people' and 'ghost hunters' to 'scaremongers' and other appellations, including 'charlatans' (Duckett, 1991). The Warrens' usual modus operandi has them arriving at a 'haunted' house where ghost and poltergeist hijinks are blown into incredible accounts of 'demonic possession.' Soon the horrific tales become chapters or entire books touting the Warrens' 'cases,' such as the Amityville 'horror,' (Amityville, New York, 1975, 1976) and the Snedeker family haunting (Southington, Connecticut, 1986, 1988). In the latter case, in addition to Lorraine Warren, 'psychics' brought into the house (a former funeral home) included a Warren grandson and a nephew. They were soon reporting their own sightings of ghosts and other phenomena, while also denying that there was any book deal in progress. In fact, such a book did materialize (Warren and Warren et al, 1992). Alas, when I appeared on the pre-Halloween 1992 Sally Jessy Raphael show with the Warrens and Snedekers, I began an investigation that would thoroughly demolish the case (although it was hyped again later with a made for TV movie). Neighbors of the Snedekers' came on the Sally show to debunk many of the claims. One was an across-the-street resident, Kathy Altemus, who had kept a journal during the events and shared it with me when I subsequently visited Southington. The journal shed light on the ghostly occurrences. For example, 'vibrations' felt in in the house were easily explained by the passing of heavy trucks. Other events could perhaps be attributed to various passersby mentioned in the journal as 'pulling pranks on the 'haunted house' (Altemus 1988, 92).

Certain other incidents including visiting nieces being groped by 'an unseen hand' turned out to have been caused by the Snedekers' son 'Steven' (as he is called in the book). He confessed to police that he had fondled the girls as they slept. He used drugs and was diagnosed as schizophrenic (Nickell 1995, 133, 139). While there is no convincing evidence that demons were at work in the house, the arrival of the Warrens, with their publicity-seeking actions, convinced some people otherwise. Their book, written by a professional horror tale writer and timed for Halloween release and promotion, was a travesty. It represented the worst of the 'psychic' approach to ghost hunting. As such evidence demonstrates whether alleged psychics claim to enter a 'trance' state, like Holzer's favorite mediums, Ethel Meyers and Sybil Leek (Holzer, 1991), or whether they rely on 'channeling tools' such as a Ouija board, dowsing rod, or psychic pendulum as others prefer (Belanger 2005, 17) psychics have a poor track record. They typically offer unsubstantiated, even unverifiable claims, or information that can be gleaned from research sources or from knowledgeable persons by 'cold reading' (an artful method of fishing for information). Alternatively, the psychic may simply make a number of pronouncements, trusting that the credulous will count the apparent hits and ignore, or interpret appropriately, the misses. Still, not all such offerings are insincere. Those who fancy themselves psychics may exhibit traits associated with a 'fantasy-prone' personality, a designation for an otherwise normal person's heightened propensity to fantasize. Some field research I have done shows a correlation between the number and intensity of ghostly experiences on the one hand and the number of exhibited traits associated with fantasy-proneness on the other (Nickell 2000)."

FYI Mr. Nickell, I have been inside Ringwood Manor and some of those rooms in the summer time on a tour were freezing cold with no explanation. Not to mention that we felt as if we were being watched and were uncomfortable. There is nothing wrong with having a fantasy oriented mind at times, the latter being a dull mind is not much fun. And so in part, I wish many people had the fantasy-oriented mind over the dull. Life is meant to be lived, experienced, and enjoyed. There are things we just can't always explain, as we are just a small piece to a larger puzzle. Who are we to assume we know and can explain everything on God's green earth? Give me a break! This information is crucial to explaining exactly what Hans had to put up with. Whether you are a believer, skeptic or somewhere sitting on that paranormal fence, Hans knew what he believed and didn't believe and made that abundantly clear.

Chapter Thirteen:
(Lucky Thirteen as Hans would say)

Life Abroad

Catherine recalls a moment in Ireland where Hans joined a travel group to do a haunted house tour and lecture. They had Sybil Leek, a well-known and respected medium, with them. "While traveling on a train, Sybil had a pet "snake" in a white basket. This snake went wherever she went as we continued on to explore many other sites in Ireland. So we are in the train compartment, I am lying down and the basket is on the floor. I open my eyes and there is this thing staring right at me! It scared the heck right out of me, and not only that but when driving we had to make pit stop so "snaky could do a run" on the grass. Don't ask me! One night while in the hotel we get a frantic call from Sybil! Snaky got stuck between the toilet seat and the bowl in the back. So guess who had to rescue it? Snaky was put in the tub and then proceeded to shed its skin. Lovely, I thought to myself, just lovely. Hans will tackle an odd foul smelling ghost, but not a pet snake! Go figure."

Through Hans, Catherine was able to gain recognition of her ability to be part of the paranormal world along with being quite an extraordinary artist. The Friday, November 8, 1963 headline of the *New York World Telegram and Sun* read: "She Hunts Ghosts, Paints 'Em' by Maxine Lowry." Here is the content of the article from over five decades ago. It includes the part I love about my Russian grandfather who dabbled in the un-dead.

Catherine: Fifty years ago, people didn't believe in radio because they didn't understand it; they still don't understand it, but now they accept it. I think the same is true of ghosts. In twenty years or so people will accept ghosts too.

Reporter: Whether other people believe in ghosts or not, Mrs. Holzer does even though she's never seen one.

Catherine: When you try to break something apart logically and scientifically and there's still no answer, then it has to be something you can't explain like a ghost. (Few apparitions are ever sighted,) You have to be very sensitive to see a ghost.

Reporter: But Mrs. Holzer has heard enough haunting experiences to convince her of their reality. Emotionally stable, intelligent people have reported broken clocks that started ticking again, footprints in a dusty attic where no one has been, loud noises that have no explainable origin. The slim, attractive young brunette married into the ghost-hunting business. Her husband, Hans Holzer, is a psychic investigator who has been studying the supernatural for more than twenty years.

Catherine: I vaguely knew about it before, but because my husband was involved in it, I became involved.

Reporter: Her earliest brush with the occult was as a child in northern Italy where she was born. A countess by birth, she is a direct descendant of Catherine the Great of Russia and is related to many of Europe's royal families. The family shared a "dark, spooky, medieval castle" with a count that was interested in the supernatural.

Catherine: He pestered the spirits with séances until they got mad at him. One day a hand came down from the ceiling and slapped him across the face. That ended his investigations.

Reporter: All ghosts aren't found in old castles or run down mansions, Mrs. Holzer said. Some haunted places around New York that her husband has investigated include St. Mark's in the Bouwerie Church, a rock in the backwoods of Connecticut, and even a new apartment building on the East Side. Wherever there's a ghost, Mrs. Holzer explained, there's sure to have been an unusual event, often a murder or an unnatural death sometime in the past.

Catherine: The ghosts have some very strong emotional or physical tie to the place and he keeps reliving some happening over and over.

Reporter: If Holzer's investigation convinces him that the haunting has no logical explanation, he calls in a medium to hold a séance and exorcise the restive spirit. Helping her husband with his ghost hunts has encouraged Mrs. Holzer to further pursue her hobby of painting. She has done oils of several of the haunted houses and these plus other paintings. Many of the paintings illustrate Holzer's new book, *Ghost Hunter*. Mrs. Holzer has been seriously interested in painting since childhood, "but Hans pushed me to do the haunted houses and exhibit and sell my paintings." Although she's a keen student of ghostly goings-on, Mrs. Holzer has no desire to live in a haunted house.

Catherine: I know about the subject but if anything like that ever happened to me, I'd be frightened to death.

Another article soon published again on the fascinating life Hans and Catherine were leading. The life that created more public paranormal awareness mixing in with art and culture.

The December 5, 1963 headline of *The Daily News* read: "On the Town" by Charles McHarry. "Spook Paintings, anyone for art today? Catherine Buxhoeveden, who claims to be the great great great granddaughter of Catherine the Great, is showing her paintings at the John J. Myers Gallery. The oils are mostly concerned with ghost and ghostly subjects that the artist says were inspired by psychic explorations in haunted houses. Many of them appear in a book authored by her husband Hans Holzer, titled *Ghost Hunter*.

A May 1, 1964 Holzer Reception in Wilmington, North Carolina: "Mrs. Edwin A Harris entertained at a formal reception in honor of Mr. and Mrs. Hans Holzer. About one hundred Wilmingtonians were present to meet the Holzers during the evening. Holzer is the noted parapsychologist who will deliver a lecture at Brogden Hall. Mrs. Holzer is the great-great-great granddaughter of Catherine the Great of Russia."

The next article is a piece of history that many of you reading can understand and is relevant to life in general and is one more example of what our generations before us went through during a time of war. Catherine was lucky to have met Hans, and together at one time, made a good team.

A May 3, 1964 headline from Wilmington, North Carolina read: "German Bombs Once Threatened Countess" by Arnold Kirk. Tilting her head to let a soft ocean breeze caress her delicate face, the young woman gazed through blue-grey eyes at the erratic flight of gulls flocking overhead in the bright April sky. She smiled, revealing flawless rows of evenly chiseled teeth, then frowned as the birds suddenly darted out of sight behind a row of sun bleached cottages extending southward from the towering Blockade Runner Motor Hotel. Practitioners of the guessing game would have supposed the young woman to be a professional model...or perhaps, a beautiful actress seeking retreat from the noisy streets of New York or some other distant place. Indeed, few would have guessed her to be the wife of one of the world's most famous ghost hunters. Catherine Holzer, the vivacious 24-year-old wife of parapsychologist Hans Holzer, tapped her immaculately groomed fingernails gently across the cover of a note pad as she recalled her early childhood in the picturesque Austrian Alps. Born Catherine Buxhoeveden, the youngest of five children of an Austrian count and his Parisian wife, the young woman seemed destined from birth to become in some way connected with the supernatural world of the life beyond. Her birthplace, a medieval castle nestled high in the mountains near Tyrol, Italy, which was then a part of Austria, was supposed to have been haunted by restless spirits from a century past.

> Catherine: At night you could hear them walking about in the castle. There were tall trees all about and it was as if you were all alone there in the darkness.

But whatever fears this young Cathy and her family had of ghosts quickly gave way to a more tangible danger at the outbreak of World War II.

> Catherine: The Germans came first. For no reason at all, their airplanes would swoop down from the sky and start dropping bombs and shooting at the castle with machine-guns. Once, a bomb landed at the exact spot where my mother and sister had been sitting in the yard just a few minutes before.

During another bombing raid, a deadly German aim sent a bomb crashing through the roof of the castle to land, still intact, in a room where the family had gathered for shelter. "If the bomb had exploded," Mrs. Holzer directed her remark to a reporter, "I would not be here talking to you today." She said the only way the family could move about in the mine-laden streets of nearby Florence were for each child to walk in the footsteps placed by their father.

But the end of the war brought no comfort for the Buxhoeveden family. Italy's political unrest made many families of foreign descent targets of threats from fascists who at that time plundered and killed without just provocation. In 1947, the family boarded an old converted troop transport ship for the long journey to America. A year later, Catherine's father died at the family's new home on Long Island, New York. Despite her tomboyish antics, Cathy Buxhoeveden continued her life-long pursuit of becoming a skilled artist and enrolled at Hunter College (*Trivia: My sister Nadine later attended this college and I attended the Fashion Institute of Technology in New York as Catherine had before*), where she became an ardent student of the brush and canvas. Still in her teens, the young woman's paintings gained wide acclaim throughout areas of the Southeast. Owing probably to her legend-filled childhood, Catherine's favorite subjects were haunted houses. Her endeavors were rewarded in 1961, when she received an award from the Kit Kat Club in New York City. In fact, it was through this social group that Mrs. Holzer met her famous husband, who at that time was gathering information for his recently published book, *Ghost Hunter*.

"We met at a party one night," Mrs. Holzer recalled, "and when I saw Hans, I knew I had found the man I had been waiting for." If she had been waiting for a husband much unlike most men, Catherine Buxhoeveden made a wise choice by selecting Hans Holzer. "He is an extremely sensitive person," Mrs. Holzer revealed. She said her husband was particularly unlearned on such matters at automotives and making repairs to their six room apartment.

The Saturday, March 27, 1965 *New York Journal American* read: "Countess Catherine Buxhoeveden, who specializes in painting haunted houses she visits with her author-husband, Hans Holzer, of

Ghost Hunter fame, has designed the cover for her husband's new record album, "Ghosts I've Met," which is also the name of his new book due in May from Bobbs-Merrill. *(See I told you he was trying to get that off, off way off Broadway musical.)* The album features interviews with witnesses to uncanny phenomena, and excerpts from actual séances Ghost Hunter Hans Holzer has arranged as part of his investigations of haunted houses and poltergeists the world over."

The September 30-October 13, 1966 issue: Park East Thursday, October 6. Art and Artists by Betsy Polier. "Catherine Buxhoeveden, wife of parapsychologist Hans Holzer, is exhibiting a series of paintings and drawings, "Haunted Houses and Other Things," at the New York Hilton. There's nothing ghostly about the artist's technique; it's solidly academic and in some cases (notably, in the smaller canvases) quite professional. Some of the houses, for example Skreene Castle, Ireland, do look haunted, though, and that's to the artists' credit. Also included in the show are paintings of Paris and Ireland as well as St. Marks in the Bowerie in New York. If you like amateur landscape painting with lots of atmosphere, you'll like this show."

September 27 to October 25, 1970, Man and the Machine: An Exhibit of Graphics by J White, L. Paz, G. Gubeck, C. Buxhoeveden, P. Allen and a Computer. "Helping her famous husband with his psychic investigations has given Catherine much of her inspiration. Her exploration of pen and ink expresses a feeling for the intimacy of things to come, a role which the artist must assume in such a technical society to help humanize what is constantly changing."

This was the last article I acquired from Catherine, but others followed as Hans was interviewed several times by the media, radio shows, and is published in the Who's Who in America books. I incorporated them into the book pretty neatly, I think. Hans was no stranger to interviews by this point, as more would follow his career and life. The Amityville murders would put him on a new plateau of writing. The next article shows a very good explanation on Hans' eating preference as a die-hard vegan. Many people have a misconception of a vegetarian. Some can eat cheese while others can eat eggs and so on. Hans below is described as one of the strictest of strict vegetarians on this planet. Here you see the crumbling between Hans and Catherine, as she begins to show signs of annoyances with Hans and differences of lifestyles. Folks, the honeymoon is over.

The Saturday, March 15, 1975 headline of the New York Post read: "At Home with Hans and Catherine Holzer" by Jeremy Tallmer. You might say of Hans Holzer that the supernatural is his oyster, except that, as a good vegetarian, Holzer does not eat oysters. Or fish. Or meat. Or eggs. Much to his wife's despair. Well, we'll get to that. In any event he's the fellow who has made a career of ghosties and ghoulies and things that go bump in the dark, as prolific lecturer and writer on every sort of 'paranormal occurrence' from ESP to haunted houses. Also, witchcraft, known to the cognoscenti as Wicca. *Heather: Confessions of a Witch* is his thirty-seventh book now in print, but the 55-year-old Holzer, not exactly one of your shrinking violets, shrugs off such productivity. Bouncing between phone calls at home on an afternoon early in his week, he remarked: "when you have one successful book, somebody wants another one. It's like mushrooms." Home is 'a museum' of a six-room apartment on Riverside Drive, its walls a forest of his collection of Greek, Roman, Egyptian statuettes interspersed with paintings by his wife Catherine. They've been married thirteen years; are the parents of Nadine, 11 1/2, and Alexandra, 4 next month; have lived here since just before the arrival of Nadine. "A co-op? Oh no. Over my dead body, if you'll pardon the expression. Rent-controlled." Holzer was born in Vienna in 1920, son of a businessman; came here with his parents in the 1930s; lived "for eighteen years in Forest Hills and hated every minute of it." Other Holzerisms: "I'm a professional nonconformist...uninfluencable, unemployable, and unpredictable... Anything that'll bust a few shirts, I'm for." *(This is what would get him into trouble... his lovely way with words.)*

"He and his wife met through a conjunction of interest in astrology, theatricals, and art. She is, or was, Countess Catherine Buxhoeveden, born 1939 in Merano, Italy, brought to America in 1946 to be raised on Long Island. "I remember," says Catherine Holzer, "when the Fascists came to where we were living outside Florence, in the hills, and said: 'You have so much time to leave this house.' I remember that very clearly." Also an artillery shell rolling slowly down all the steps without exploding. Her father, an architect and builder of Riviera hotels, was of a line of Baltic nobility stretching back, it is said, to Catherine the Great. He has been dead a quarter-century. Her French mother, very much alive, is, like son-in-law Holzer, a vegetarian."

The article goes on to talk about Hans' new book. "Heather the Witch, just one of your nice little girls from small town, Ohio, who comes to the big town (this one) and forth with flowers into a high priestess of sex, television and Wicca in roughly equal proportions. "The first and only time I have told somebody else's story," said Holzer. She came up to him at one of his lectures; he put her down on tape, later destroyed, *(sounds like Mission Impossible)*. How, then, to prove her existence? "My word." And if there are those who refuse to believe? "I say: 'Your welcome.' I did show my publisher (Mason/Charter) release from the lady, but that paper is very secret." Has he heard from the lady since the book came out? "Yes, two sentences: 'It's fine. Be sure nobody finds me.'" Well then. Has the lady ever been to dinner in his apartment? "No, never." Has your wife ever seen her? "Never. I keep my business out of this house."

The article shifts towards Catherine before it ends. "We have people in about once a month. Eight or nine, perhaps as many as fifteen during the holidays. It's difficult, yes, very difficult, doing vegetarian and non-vegetarian all together. It doesn't make always for a happy wife. I get very bitchy at times. If only he ate eggs, I wouldn't mind it so much. When you run out of ideas you can make a whole meal out of an omelet." "I will not eat a dessert," said her husband, "that has one egg in it."

Trivia, to this day, when I cook for our family, he always asks me, "Darling, does it have eggs in it?", and I lower my eyes and crinkle up as I politely mutter under my breath, "Nooooo," and walk away. I, too, cook both vegetarian and non-vegetarian for all of these folks so I can feel my mother's past cooking pain. Back to the rest of the article...

"He will cook an egg for one of our daughters," said Mrs. Holzer, extending a sigh, "but he won't carve meat." "Meat contains all the problems of the animal, and the adrenalin at time the animal is killed," said Mr. Holzer. "An egg, well, that is more a moral issue, the sacrosanct status of life." Does he eat butter? "Yes. There's no killing involved with butter." So to make a long story short, Mrs. Holzer does the regular shopping and Mr. Holzer does the special shopping twice a week at health-food stores. *(He thinks the health-food business is a racket, a scandal, but that's another matter.) Here comes the part about my Parisian grandmother, whom I just adore! Rosine Claire's French Gourmet Vegetarian Cookbook is a work by* Mrs. Holzer's mother coming out in September, with illustrations by [Catherine Holzer]. One delectable recipe in it is the appetizer of Mushrooms in Green Sauce with which the meal often starts at the Holzers. "Because I don't have meat that often, I don't mind spending the money and might have one of my favorites, veal alla marsala. Then the vegetables: a string beans mignotte, which is half beans and half zucchini, and, for color contrast, broiled tomatoes topped with parmesan cheese, bread crumbs and chopped black olives. A salad, you name the salads and we have them." "My husband hardly drinks, but I love wine. With this meal, a rose. And, for dessert, Cherries Jubilee, flamed at the table." Holzer stretched his legs. "When my wife has people in to dinner, it's a candlelight dinner, it has style," he said. "She's a perfectionist. I am forced to put on shoes. It's real rough stuff. Of course I don't put on a necktie. Not yet." *And there you have it Ladies and Gentlemen, the Hans we knew and still know and love dearly.*

Chapter Fourteen:
Childhood Memories

Hans as a father was always responsible and attentive doing his best as only he knew how. Certainly in the Holzer household there is such a word as 'Holzerisms,' as mentioned above, in which it was his way or the highway. Regardless of 'Holzerisms' running amuck in the apartment, there were many memorable moments to share....

The Flea Market King

Growing up in Manhattan was great and always surrounded our family with chaos and noise. Aside from the typical parks, playgrounds, theaters, museums, uptown, downtown, way down town to the village, China Town, Little Italy, there was one place in particular that was the playground for Hans. As a grown man, he still kept a Sunday ritual of flea marketing going for several decades.

The flea market was held on the Upper West Side in the 1970s on a basketball court. It was great because it was fenced in and once you entered, you felt as if you were surrounded by a bazillion artifacts and odd strangers selling something one of a kind. Of course, I went on this adventure with Hans as often as possible. I always anticipated coming away with a new item that I could treasure and hide for safe keeping. He was always very good like that. When we walked into the front gate, he clenched my hand twice and that was his signal to say, "let's go and seek." We went diagonal, we zig zagged, we spun around until our heads were light as feathers.

Then, after thirty minutes of flying about the maze of treasures, Hans would spot something. Something to him that could quite possibly be a rare find. Perhaps he saw a mystical chalice? Maybe it was an antique that came from the Ming Dynasty? The Holy Grail? What could it be? Tightening his grip once again on my little hand, we flew like Mary Poppins across courtside. There in front of the longest table I had ever seen were the most bizarre antiques and masks imaginable. A woman sat behind this table, staring at Hans. Let the games begin!

"And what is it, sir, that you're looking for today?" she asked in an evil like way. I began to retreat behind Hans' tall shadow hoping she'd go away. Instead Hans swung me back around and continued on with his pursuit. "Madame, I see you have a mask here and I would like to know it's price!" bellowed out Hans. The old woman grinned slyly as she rose from her chair. A three-legged chair mind you, and I skirted around Hans to get a better glimpse. Oh she was scary, I tell you! If it wasn't for her three-legged blind dog, then I might have run off in fright. I began patting the little grey haired dog as Hans and the old woman began the bargaining. "I'll sell it to you for fifteen dollars as I can see you know your artifacts." Hans didn't respond right away as he proceeded to pick up the most heinous looking mask I had ever seen. It was red and jewels were over its cut out, pear-shaped eyes, and had a pointy protruding nose. If I didn't know any better, I think it scowled at me! "I'll give you seven dollars ma'am, as you see I know where this is from." The old woman didn't know what to do. Perhaps she never encountered such a man like this before. After all, Hans was the king of the flea markets in all of Upper West Side Manhattan. The old woman tried again at her fate. "Clearly, sir, you can see all the detailed work in this mask. Surely you feel it has a worth of twelve dollars?" "What?" I said to myself. "I thought she said fifteen." And then I began to understand what he was doing. Again Hans didn't respond right away. I slowly stood back up from the dog as I looked on to see what would happen next. The stakes were high. "Madame, I will give you seven dollars or nothing at all," answered Hans. I couldn't believe my ears. He was really pushing it. Then the old woman lowered one brow, muttered something under her breath, and, sitting back down, she grabbed a small white plastic bag. "Will that be all, sir?" As Hans firmly placed the seven dollars down, he tipped his hat to her and said, "Yes!"

This went on for many Sundays thereafter and my sister and I started to appreciate the art of flea market shopping. Nadine would join Hans on occasion, hence taking the torch from myself. I veered off that path as a rebellious teen, and entering art school, taking on other interests. But, from time to time when Hans returned from one of his Sunday adventures, I would find a little something strewn across my bed. Perhaps one Sunday I'd find a new cross necklace. Another Sunday I'd find a round shaped jeweled ring. Usually too large to wear on my bony piano like fingers, so I placed them on a chain and wore it that way. I began to look forward to Hans' return on Sundays like a kid in a candy store. This was my treat and I loved it so. It was indeed a rare and odd outing, but showed a father's love just the same. Hans didn't run and catch ball or skip jump rope with his girls. He didn't play ring-a-round a rosy or piggy back. What Hans did was shower his girls with flea market jewelry, stuffed animals, stories, and anything else he felt we would enjoy. Hans did walk with us to the Riverside Drive Park and push us on a swing. Hans played the piano and sang songs to us while in turn educating us to play the piano. Hans entertained in the evening, always including his children as centerpieces and his pride and joy. Here is where the age difference between my sister and I stood out. She would do the disappearing act and I was left standing, frozen, pulled into Hans' magical atmospheric environment. But to tell the truth, I rather enjoyed it as I looked up at him as a magical person who happened to chase ghosts and be a bit eccentric at times. That was Hans and that was just fine by me!

Just Out and About

Whenever Hans went anywhere, he'd have a certain way in crossing the streets. The elevator doors opened and I was done staring at my shoes to avoid eye contact with other riders. You know, those neighbors that seem so odd and giant-like when you're little? Relief would come as the doors opened and the elevator floor would bounce a couple of times and settle along the wires in the shaft. When he went out, it was always with his hat. His head would bow down as if to greet the Queen, and then we were off like horses at a racing track. He'd grab hold of my hand tightly as we flew through the 'push your way out and hurry before you go back the way you came' doors. Now we were on our block, which is a very long block that always seemed like an eternity to walk. It really is the size of two city blocks put together. I assume a cruel joke from the city engineer? Down the street we'd walk, passing brownstone after brownstone. I'd marvel on how old and beautiful they all were. Sometimes I'd imagine what it would be like living in one? I liked the notion that you could just trot down some steps and you were home. No elevators, no doorman, just you and your home. The street would be lined with car after car on both sides. I'd look at the different colors and shapes and really, really bad parking jobs. Then the time came to stop. The street corner was upon us, and the Hans grip became tighter. I think at one point I became dizzy.

Back then our cross walks had the actual yellow square boxes up on a post that read in red "Don't Walk" and in green "Walk." I always thought that was so cool and would tempt the sign, crossing the street as it began to blink several times. A true New Yorker would know this to be the warning sign you get before you're about to get hit by oncoming traffic. But today I was going out with my father so that would not be the case. "WALK." My body was still standing on the street corner now on West End Avenue, as my father again flew us across the street to the other side. It wouldn't be until seconds later that I caught up with myself again and met my father as a whole.

Riding the bus with him was not as exciting as the actual walking experience, but it was necessary in order to get across town. All my doctor appointments were always on the East Side. *Now that I think about it, that was really dumb. What, they couldn't find anyone good on the West Side? Us West Siders' and them East Siders', well, there was a difference. Especially when I was a teen and bar-hopping. Boy, there was definitely a difference between that crowd compared to ours, but that is another story.* Cab riding with Hans was also an adventure. Remember I told you a few chapters back about Hans' navigating in the car? Well, this was no different. Now, when we rode taxi cabs we always targeted the yellow checkered cabs with the pull out seats behind the driver. No seat belts and complete and utter dangerous freedom. But man could those cabs fly through the streets of New York. I would stick my head out the window like a puppy dog, frigid or sultry hot, and just blink away smiling. Of course, Hans would lean into the plastic divider with the holes in it to speak with the driver. "Sir, would you kindly mind turning down the heat? We're melting back here. Thank you." And that was that. I could have died a thousand deaths like my mother of embarrassment versus her stage fright! I also used to peel those yellow and black taxi cab stickers off the ripped blue vinyl backing and move them around and misplace them in the cab. You should have seen what we used to do to the buses, but then again, I think I'll just leave that one alone. So, there you have it… a day out and about with the Ghost Hunter. Hopefully getting through it quick enough to survive the trip back home. Up that linked two block mass, through those revolving panic attack doors, past the door-man, into that shaky elevator, away from those odd neighbors and back into my safe haven of a home… home, where African voodoo masks hung in abundance, crosses and gargoyle statues greeted you, and that familiar smell of the Holzer house. Ah, it was good to be home. That is what Hans and Catherine created for us, which I will always appreciate and gently reflect upon as I, too, change and grow in my own life.

Chapter Fifteen

CATHERINE COMES OUT, VOLLEYBALL, AND THE GHOST OF MRS. LERNER

Catherine Comes Out

When you live in a pre-war building that takes up two whole blocks and has two streets for it, you can bet there are a lot of neighbors living there. Of course, in our building they didn't have the number "thirteen" as a floor. No, you went from twelve to fourteen, which always seemed to bug me. My father would usually look at it and snicker behind his breath something like, "13...13... it's a good number. What's wrong with 13?" My mother made some friends and some of them were quite interesting characters. There was the single, bitter but fun divorcee with two children out of control. I always felt bad for her. She was a clothing designer and one time made me this dark grey-striped flock of Seagull's flap shirt that you weren't suppose to wash in the washer machine. The attention span of my youth was limited. I used the washer machine! Hence it became a top for one of my barbie dolls.

Other friends who were down the hall from us was a gay couple that Catherine befriended. The one woman was a children's book writer and is still writing children's books. I remember the first book she gave me, signed. I loved her. She was one of the funniest, French, gay woman I have ever known. Not that I knew many, but if I had, she'd be it! My father was oblivious to all of this fraternizing and had no clue what was to come. In a lot of ways I already knew, but for him, it blindsided him. One time we were in her apartment, hanging out and cooking. It was both of the women, Catherine and I.

Volleyball Break

I have no clue where my sister was at the time, but I surmise playing volleyball. At that time Nadine was eating, sleeping and dreaming volleyballs. In high school she was always winning awards, trophys and was such a darn great athlete. At one point she made the try-outs for The Empire State Games and did a little traveling with them. One time my father was complaining because there was a huge, dirty white netted bag bulging from out of the corner of my sister's room. He needed to know what everything was in every one's rooms. He was just that way, nosy. "Alex, Alex come here. Go into your sister's room and find out what that bag is," Hans would demand. So, in I went and opened up the stupid bag of what seemed like twenty volleyballs pouring down on me. After I got up and out from under the volleyball heap, I turned to Hans and said, "and what shall you have me do with them, these cruel and guilty, vicious balls?" With that he turned around and stormed out of her room, pissed off at me. Oh, well, I thought it was funny. For Hans, funny was a different kind of funny. The jokes he'd crack were about people in history or a ghost he came across that did or said something absurd. This was not my idea of funny, but in any case these were his rules and it was his house.

Back to Catherine

Getting back to the women and that time in their apartment. So, they are cooking dinner and having a splendid glass of French wine. I sat, listening to their conversations and laughter, chomping on celery stalks. All of a sudden, out of the blue, a question is asked of me and at that time I was clueless to its content and meaning.

Now that I think about it, it boils my blood a bit that my mother didn't say anything because I now have children. It is nothing against

these women in that room in any way. It is actually my mother that I
would be directing this at. In the early 1980s, conversations were very
different, and in my family's case, the way we lived was always very
different than how many of my classmates lived. We had lots of par-
ties, traveled, knew well-known people and had many beautiful pieces
of art in our home on display. Not to mention darn ghosts everywhere!
When Catherine left us, much of the art went with her, but she was
not cruel about it. It took years of going back and forth, claiming her
items. Hans, well, he just rolled with it and was just happy to see her.
A true romantic at heart. They were very amicable that way, and for
that I think my sister and I will always appreciate and have respect.

Back to that question for me. "Alex, what do you think a male
private part looks like?"

There was silence as the three women looked amongst themselves waiting for my response. Being that I was never at a loss
for words, right away answered the one who asked. Mind you,
I really hadn't a clue as to what or why she would ask that and I
certainly didn't know the correct answer. This, much to Catherine's
silent facial relief. My answer: "Well, I believe it looks sort of like
my celery stalk and maybe it's green too!" All three women burst
out in laughter as I nervously chuckled along, rolling my eyes side
to side in relief that I said something amusing. One of the woman
said looking down at her cutting board in her heavy French accent,
"Okay, Alex, okay, good answer" and with that I was let off the hook
for the rest of the evening on the male genitalia! I think they were
just being silly with me and, well, I wasn't so ha ha. A male's you
know what to them, must have been like a useless device, foreign
for their purpose in life. That's how it went with the friends at
Riverside Drive.

Catherine on her first lesbian relationship: "In 1971 just prior
to you being born, I met a woman (she is still part of our family,
happily married, and close to all of us) through a friend of Mother

and Hans who lived in the same building. This woman's daughter and Nadine were attending the French school, the Lycee Francais. A year after we met we became lovers, to the surprise of ourselves and ultimately the husbands. That relationship lasted for over twelve years and to this day we still have a strong bond."

If I knew this back then, I'd still feel the same way as I do today. This woman is a second mother to Nadine and I, as we affectionally would call her our 'Parisian' mother. She's wonderful as is her husband and daughter with whom Nadine retains a close relationship with.

At age thirteen, I had discovered two incredible things. One was that singer Chaka Kahn and a band member from the musical group Kiss were living in my building. Once, I was outside playing in front of the building, and out Chaka came with a wade of gorgeous hair. It wasn't until she came right up to my friend and I that we could see her beautiful face and hear her luxurious, raspy voice. She was kind and spoke with us for a few moments. She was holding the hand of her little child getting ready to cross the street and go to Riverside Park. I told her that I loved to sing and she told me not to give up if I truly believed and enjoyed it. I mentioned I loved her and her album and she offered to sign it for me. What a thrill to have met her. A true talented and gifted singer with a song titled, "Aint' Nobody," was forever my favorite. I never got to see the guitarist, but my sister was always in awe of him, living a few floors below us on the same level. We were on the same side of the building so our windows lined up. You could open up that window and look down at his air conditioner. What a thrill!

The second thing I discovered at age thirteen was not as glamorous or as easy to experience. I found lesbian books in my mother's bookcase and started to put two and two together. I wasn't being nosy, but then again I was, just a little. I loved books and their jacket designs. My mother had already designed a few of them for Hans' books, so I became interested in the way each book looked, felt and its title. I liked — and still do — the way a crisp new piece of paper smells! I innocently stumbled upon the lesbian books and put them back quickly and ran out of their room. Hans also had romantic books in his book case, but I don't think the two topics ever quite meshed!

One night Catherine had a talk with me explaining that she and Hans were to separate. It would be left up to me with whom I wanted to live. I cried, she cried, and we just agreed to always be with each other no matter what. My sister was well ahead of me with college, work and relationships, and that darn volleyball! My father continued writing books, and my mother worked as a facilities manager and, from time to time, doing her art. The Holzer house that was once bustling with activity of human existence became a quiet place for the dead to rest. It was the first time the four of us went our own way regardless of our age ranges. I grew up quickly that year.

The Ghost of Mrs. Lerner

Around the time I was in the seventh grade there was this one neighbor, Mrs. Lerner, who would always come by and bother my father for a cup of something. No, she wasn't THAT type of neighbor, sickies! She was alone, aging, and in need of attention. She had the apartment next to us. When you got off of the elevator on our floor, to the right was Mrs. Lerner and to the left was us, then a long hallway that continued as an L shape. Our women neighbors, as well as others, lived along the hall and at the end. The doorbell would ring and Hans would go to answer it and see Mrs.

Lerner humped over, in her beige housecoat, sheepishly looking at my father. Sometimes, she seemed to me like a lost puppy and other times just sad.

When I would come home from school, she'd be sitting in the building's lobby, watching as the elevator doors opened and closed. I always felt bad for her, and seeing how Hans was always helpful with her, I decided to do so myself. I began asking her if she wanted me to take her upstairs to her door. She smiled and accepted gratefully. I knew I was doing something right. When my father told me of her passing, I was very upset and disturbed by the news. She didn't have much family and never let anyone in her home. She was the nervous type and I can't say now that I blame her. Alone and aging in the city? That is very intimidating to say the least.

One day after school I was in the living room watching television as I always did. From the corner of my eye, I saw a woman come through the front door and walk right into my father's office. I sat there at first not really believing what had just occurred, and continued watching my program, The Edge of Night I believe it was. Remember that one? The next day it happened again. This time I turned around to look. But the woman was gone. Later on I told my father about it and he confirmed for me that I had just witnessed the ghost of Mrs. Lerner and she was probably looking for him to borrow something.

Other Ghostly Presences

Sometimes in the wee hours of the night, things would be in my room. I can recall a couple of instances where I was visited by a presence from another time and place. The peak times of these happenings would occur when Hans would return from a hunt. I suppose sometimes a lost ghost would cling onto Hans. The bundle of energy and his openness towards the afterlife made anything possible.

Once, on a school night, I was awakened by an odd sensation that I was being watched. Heavily breathing under my covers, I began to sweat. What, or *WHO*, the heck was in my room and could it please just go the away? On top of my entertainment stand was a huge three foot life saver coin can. It began to rattle and shake. I was still buried beneath my covers like a petrified deer caught in a headlight. A warm and buzzing sensation came over my entire being as I felt hands move over my body. Then it all just stopped. I remained under those covers until I heard my sister turn on the shower and morning light poured into my windows. What relief and confusion I felt! I looked at that can and made the decision to throw it out! Just like the TV in the movie *Poltergeist*!

On another occasion my sister had gone out for the night unbeknownst to me. She'd tell Hans and then off she'd go like a wild wolf out on the prowl. I am sure she had a volleyball or two with her! In any case, I had left my chambers (bedroom) to go ask her a question. I have no idea where Catherine was at this time, as she and Hans were barely still together. You could hear the typewriter keys being tapped on as Hans was the mad typist in the evening hours. I knocked on my sister's door and heard nothing. Then I noticed underneath that the light was off and realized that she must have gone out. I opened the door and sure enough, she was not there. So I closed it, the thoughtful sibling that I was, and went back to my lair. Not more than a few seconds later, there were three knocks at my door. "Who is it?" I called out. Getting no response, I went to the door and pressed my cheek to it. It was as cold as a winter day and I will never forget it. I suddenly became frightened and backed away from the door. Gulping what was left of moisture in my dried up throat, I decided to forge ahead and turn the knob. At this point, being in a horror film would have been preferable because at least then my lines could be re-written along with my scene! "I will not die, I will not die! I may trip, but I will not die!" I turned the cold knob and counted to three under my breath. At first it wouldn't move. Then I tried again and it was loose. I flung open the door and like an idiot, stood there looking down the empty hall. Then, a cold breeze passed and vanished as the heat from the hall returned back into my skin. I suppose I had disturbed something resting in my sister's room being it was unoccupied at the time, or something was in the apartment playing games on me. Luckily it never happened again.

Then there was what I call the 'Case of The Missing Black Cloak.' As a kid sometimes you save your favorite Halloween costumes in case you want to use them again for another year. I had about three cloaks in my bottom dresser drawer saved just for that reason. One was a red satin devil cloak, one was a black witches' cloak, and the third, a basic vampire collared cloak. One night, after completing my homework, I had gone into the living room to watch some TV before Hans came in and dominated the room. It wasn't until

I was thirteen that I had my own thirteen-inch TV. That was some day! *I'll put it to you this way, my eldest two children had their first bedroom TVs at ages FOUR and SIX! Times, they are a changin'.* I had to go to the bathroom, which was passed my bedroom. As I was passing my room, one of my black cloaks was standing up over the opened bottom drawer. I thought I was going to have a heart attack! I didn't know what to do so I ran into the bathroom, slammed shut the door, and locked it! In those apartments, the doors were made of real wood and metal and had major locks on them. I waited as, at that point, I could not pee. I waited for I don't know how long, ten, twenty seconds. Then I opened the door and peeked out. As I did, I saw that the cloak was gone and the drawer was pushed in. I thought I was losing my mind. As I entered my room there was a strange odor, and as I was noticing that, it went away. Needless to say what I did to the life saver coin can, I did with the cloak. It was a nice one too.

The whole time growing up in that household, I never was in fear of being in danger, but I always felt that there were many presences around me at times. If there were any foul ghosts, I believe that the good spirits who are here to protect us pushed them out and kept all of us safe. I bet there was a waiting list for all ghouls and ghosts to get into the Holzer house but to no avail. Too many bouncer guides and angels at the front door, turning them away for bad identification! Just like a lost puppy or kitten can follow an individual home, so can a ghost!

Chapter Sixteen:

INTERVIEW WITH A VAMPIRE...

NO EXCUSE ME, I MEAN HANS HOLZER

Part I:

This next article is a great conversation piece between a reporter and Hans. It provides a lot of insight at a time in Hans' life when things were at a high point. Of course today, many things in this piece have changed including some of his views in the scientific arena — an arena he is pushing strongly these days while still keeping his faith and spirituality intact. I believe we are all allowed to change our views if we have learned something new from the original lesson. I don't believe in flip flopping in order to gain others respect or go by the way of the wind at that particular moment. This article is from Merilan News.

Merlian News: When did you first become interested in the esoteric world?

Hans: I was about eight years old and I became interested because I had an uncle named Henry who was very strange. According to family, he was a wonderful man who was interested in what you call the esoteric world; ghosts, faeries, and all sorts of psychic things.

Merlian News: So tell me a little more about your uncle who sparked this interest in you.

Hans: My Uncle Henry, although he worked in his father's shop, he was deeply interested in strange things, like sleeping in an eighteenth century bed for instance, having books about ghosts and spirits and strange things had happened, and it rubbed off because he and I were very close, and I found it fascinating what he did. He would walk by the river and say, 'You see this tree over there? Well, there are faeries in that tree and you got to say hello to them,' and things like that. He was very interesting.

Merlian News: So Uncle Henry is your mother's brother?

Hans: My Uncle Henry has passed over, but the relationship seems to have continued because I have heard from him through a British medium, a number of times. And the last time I had heard from him (the medium) Philip Solomon said, 'Your Uncle Henry is here.' I wanted to make sure I was talking to my Uncle Henry, and he said 'Just a minute, he says his dog's name is Rigo,' now who on earth would know a thing like that except the person whose dog it was?

Merlian News: Have you ever personally seen or heard your mother talk to you since she passed over?

Hans: I did see my mother on one occasion. She came to my bedroom where I was sleeping and apparently my head had slipped off the pillow, which could cause a migraine, and my mother was there and I felt her hand put my head back onto the pillow.

Merlian News: How old were you then?

Hans: Well, I was in New York of course; I must have been in my forties.

Merlian News: How long had she been passed?

Hans: I think she died in 1968.

Merlian News: What was your first professional job?

Hans: I went to college at Vienna University first, studying ancient history and archeology, in addition to that numismatics. After that I spent three and a half years at Columbia University in the Far Eastern department and at the same time studying Japanese. This is during the war years. Finally I did some more work with the London College of Applied Science, where I got a Masters in comparative religion and a doctorate in philosophy. A year later I was offered a professorship at the New York Institute of Technology where I taught parapsychology for eight years. I would consider my book *Ghosts* as my most successful book in the fact that it has sold over 150 thousand (copies) so far. It's an encyclopedia of all the ghost cases that I have been involved in.

Merlian News: So you started teaching parapsychology at what age?

Hans: I was offered the professorship because of Eileen Garrett, a famous medium and psychic investigator; she and I worked together for many years, and she came to me and asked me to do an investigation of haunted houses in the eastern United States. And I got a grant to do this and the grant was renewed and renewed, and when it was all done, it was around 1960-61. She said I had to write a book, and I said, 'Eileen, it's time I got a Broadway musical going because I write Broadway musicals' and she said 'Yes, but this is important that you do a book, and you can do everything else at the same time, but I want you to write this book.' So I said I'd do it. I wrote my first book *Ghost Hunter*, it was published in 1963, and it was a great success, eventually eleven printings, probably because I was the first academically trained guy who said there are ghosts and this is what they are. Eileen has passed on, but during her lifetime we had many discussions and investigations together.

Merlian News: How many books have you had published up to date?

Hans: Actually, 138 and counting, and maybe a couple more that haven't been published yet. I'm looking for a publisher for them.

Merlian News: What books are you about to publish? Anything you can talk about now?

Hans: Well, I have my most recent book, *The Supernatural: Explaining the Unexplained*. I'm hoping to see another which is just finished called the *Spirit Connection: How the Other Side Intervenes in our Lives*, published as soon as we can settle on a publisher.

Merlian News: Are you yourself psychic?

Hans: Being a psychic investigator, and a parapsychologist, sooner or later something rubs off on you. I have been psychic to a certain degree. I've had visual experiences. My late mother appeared to me when I was in difficulty at one time, and I've heard spirit voices, voices of people who have passed over. Yes, I am psychic. I am not a professional medium, but yes I am psychic.

Merlian News: Have any of your children inherited this gift?

Hans: Actually my older daughter, Nadine, has had experiences involving a relative who has passed over who spoke to her.

I have to interrupt here. Being that my sister was eight years ahead of me, Hans was only in tune to her whereas I was too young for him to deal with on that level. He was like that when it came to his children. Catherine was better with us at a younger age and Hans was at an older age. However, I remember some of those mediums always caressing my face and saying to anyone in the room at the time, "This one is special. She has the gift," and so either Hans ignored it or knew and felt it to be normal.

It is said that those with the "gift" can detect others with the gift. Looking back on it now, those women who were friends of Hans' must have felt something about me. One sensitive person to another can perhaps detect more than one sensitive person to a harder individual. They would seem to be more closed off and distant or disconnected to feeling deeper than they perhaps would allow. It makes sense today as I have come into my own, but all that came from somewhere. I often would question Hans and ask, 'Is it a gift from above or is it inerited and only made of human cells?' Hans usually would give me a serious look as the professor who was about to lecture again. He felt it was one in the same. As we are created from something greater than one can imagine, we are also inherent of what our parents and their parents before us, in their genetic makeup pass down our way. However, I am still left to ponder that one as there are real mysteries in life and I feel this is one of them.

As for my odd occurrences at home throughout the years, I feel Hans was like a spirit magnet, attracting all those on the other side all the time. I always felt eyes on me or protected when out and about doing foolish teenage things. And, it just didn't end at home either. Sometimes when staying with Nana, I felt impressions of beings around me and occupying my space. But because I couldn't see anything, I just chalked it up to being nervous, silly, and imagining things. I rarely could sleep at night when staying with Nana. I think they follwed her too. Of course, she has the "gift" and so it goes back to the question at hand, "where does it come from?"

Merlian News: Do you have a story to tell me about your ex-wife who was somewhat psychic also?

Hans: My ex-wife did illustrations on many of my books. She, as a child, lived in a castle in Merano Tirol. She found that her bedspreads were being pulled away from her and then she found out that the house was haunted. She was no longer fearful about the whole thing. She experienced it herself.

Merlian News: Didn't Catherine the Great appear in one of your photographs?

Hans: Actually, this was during a session with a medical doctor, Andrew von Salza, who happened to have the gift of psychic photography. He was given some Polaroid film that was carefully watched, there was no one fooling around with it. He took some pictures when he came to my house for the first time and photographed my ex-wife, Countess Catherine Buxhoeveden. There appeared right next to her in white, a figure that was easily recognizable as the late empress, Catherine the Great of Russia. She was six generations removed from my Catherine.

Merlian News: Are you still investigating ghosts?

Hans: Well, no. I call ghost hunting 'investigations of alleged haunted houses.' I have done so many of them, and published quite a large amount, many cases haven't even been followed up. I only follow up places that involve some danger in the house or where it is necessary to free the entity from the house; to free the house from the ghost and the ghost from the house.

Merlian News: Are you afraid of ghosts?

Hans: I am not afraid. If you know how to handle this, you would never have any problems or danger. But there are amateur investigators who don't really know what they are doing, they sometimes get in trouble.

Merlian News: Can you give the amateurs a few hints on how not to get in trouble?

Hans: There are many well meaning young people who like to do ghost hunting. My advice is simple: find yourself a good, proven, deep trance medium and work with them. Because all the apparatus that you bring to find cold spots and all this nonsense about electronic this and electronic that is a waste of time and lack of academic knowledge.

This last paragraph is what separates Hans from any ghost hunter by today's standards. As entertaining as they are and many very good, Hans still pioneered the art of ghost hunting and therefore will forever have made his ghostly mark in this world.

Merlian News: Do you believe in reincarnation?

Hans: I had better believe in reincarnation! First of all I don't believe in believing. Because belief is the critical acceptance of something you can't prove. I believe in facts. The evidence of reincarnation is there, in a book I had written some years ago called Life Beyond.

Merlian News: How about you? Is there any particular lifetime you remember?

Hans: Yes I do, I remember very vividly a lifetime in Scotland, in connection with Glencoe. This was a terrible battle during the war between the Scottish Lairds and the German King George I.

Okay, it's me again. Thank goodness he didn't come back to be involved with another battle or we'd have a lot of misplaced ghosts wandering around asking who they can talk to for their problems. Hans and battles in the same sentence leads to disaster for sure. I mean the man couldn't operate a tennis racket let alone a sword. In any case, he was brought back to this lifetime as a ghost therapist perhaps?

Merlian News: What do you do when you're not working?

Hans: I sleep some of the time. I am not married, and I like dancing very much. I go dancing whenever the opportunity presents itself. I used to write a column about theatre and films, and I'm still very much interested in theatre and films.

Merlian News: How would films feature in this? How to get the message across?

Hans: I don't have any use for horror pictures. They are pure nonsensical fiction. I think that theatre and film are very useful to teach facts about ghosts and haunting's and parapsychology investigations, but it should be done based on fact, even when it is dramatized because it is not only the way people are entertained but they learn something.

Merlian News: What advice would you give a young person starting out in this field?

Hans: Some of the generally interested should go to school and work in philosophy; acquire a PhD in philosophy with a specialty in parapsychology. There are several universities teaching both in this country and abroad and they should also take some journalism. You need the attitude of a good journalist, 'you got to show me, I want evidence, I want witnesses.' In other words, not skepticism but cautious investigation.

Merlian News: I believe you're interested in UFOs. Have you written any or many books on them?

This is where I did differ on Hans' views as a child. Growing up I knew he would gaze across the Hudson River out into the night sky. He was looking for activity and little green men. I am not dismissing the topic of UFOs, but would welcome an opportunity in seeing one.

Hans: Some years ago I wrote a book called The *UFONAUTS: New Facts on Extraterrestrial Landings*. I am currently involved with bringing it up to date. We did another book that is going to be called *Our Space Visitors: We Are Not Alone*; all of it fully documented, based on facts of life in other galaxies and on other planets of course.

Merlian News: Do you lecture at any of these UFO conventions or give talks?

Hans: I've given lectures yes, I give lectures professionally about all of these subjects. I don't go to conferences unless I know everybody who's going to be there because unfortunately, conferences have people in them who are opposed to some of the proven things, and I don't want to get into arguments.

Merlian News: Are you still involved with the neo-pagan community?

Hans: Having written in the past three books dealing with the pagan community, with witchcraft and other forms of paganism, because that's what it is, yes. The religion is 2,000 years old or more and its still very much in evidence today. I have a book called *Witches, Warlocks, and Wizards* and it is a book that encompasses all the currently active covens or groups in the pagan movement. I myself have been initiated into the Wiccan/pagan religion three times. I am a High Priest. I am usually considered an elder statesman at the meetings. Nevertheless, I know this is a religion, and like any other religion it is a matter of the other person's opinion and acceptance.

The last piece goes off about his choices in the culinary department and his aches and pains. The last line is great because it truly depicts a Holzer. One project just won't simply do. We tend to like to have many irons in the fire.

Merlian News: How long have you been a vegetarian?

Hans: Actually, I was a vegetarian at age eleven. I was ticked off by fellow Americans at an institute, a summer school in Switzerland, falling over each other for meat, tearing it apart at lunch. After that I swore I would never touch meat again. Many years later, forty-five years ago, I turned to vegan food. Veganism means you do not touch any animal products, including eggs, cheese, and milk. It is my firm conviction through hard evidence and research that it is animal products that cause most of our illnesses.

Merlian News: Are you in good health at the present time?

Hans: I am in perfect health. I have a minor problem with a muscle in my right leg, which is going to disappear in a matter of a couple of months. In the meantime, I'm busy and I have no time to fool around with anything else except for what is positive and practical.

Merlian News: What is your next project?

Hans: I am now turning my attention to my film projects, to screenplays I have written. Not necessarily all about psychic phenomena, but about other subjects as well. I am a playwright and now I'm trying to get these to the theaters.

©*Copyright 2006 MerrynJose.com: One day, out of the blue, Merryn Jose called me after interviewing Hans for a taped interivew. She was placing me in her book as the big blue-eyed three year old running a mile a minute, showing Hans as an endearing father during her meeting with the elusive ghost hunter. After finding out what I had been doing, she phoned me and we ended up doing an article and now have become friends and will continue our relationship with the media informing them about the paranormal and my writing. This is an example of fated paths. The timing is not when you want it, but rather when it is right.*

Part II

Another noteworthy piece to discuss about Hans is an article by Rev. Laurie Sue Brockway. Here she focuses on the job at hand. Hans is allowed to again explain his beliefs through investigations and experiences. As a child I didn't have to be sat down and explained the following facts. I knew things existed because I personally experienced them whether I wanted to or not. To hear him talk to a reporter always leaves me feeling like maybe there was so much we didn't know about

Hans. If you think about it, is it even possible to know someone that well? So, I wanted to include this piece as I too have learned parts about my own father that maybe would never have surfaced unless I wrote this memoir. An example of what I was saying earlier on in the book: one path leads to another then another until, before we know what hits us, we've diverted into many different directions. It's still nice to read about Hans throughout the years as he has been written about a lot. There are too many websites and articles to even mention. When you look at the facts, he has been written about in the media for over six decades. That's a lot of print!

LSB: Hans Holzer is a real 'Ghost Buster.' The author of multiple books on the topic of disembodied spirits, those that know they are dead and those that don't (ghosts). Holzer has had amazing experiences testing the existence of ghosts and helping many of them "go home" when they get trapped in between the worlds. Obviously, his experience of things that go bump in the night transcends popular images of Casper and Halloween haunting. In fact, he speaks of ghosts and other spirit entities as if they are real people, like you and I, who are simply headed for, or living in, a different dimension. He shared with me his rather expansive understanding of the nature of spirit friends. With the world's most noted counselor to the disembodied spirits, sitting around telling ghost stories takes on new meaning.

Hans: I'm a scientist and this does not mean 'to know,' it means 'to quest for knowledge.' It's never finite. It always keeps changing and moving and you learn new things. But you do have to have standards. And scientific standards preclude me from accepting some of these fantasies. The other side tends to confirm what most religions teach. If it weren't for the facts of parapsychology, religion wouldn't have a leg to stand on. Religion takes some of the evidence, which we know in parapsychology, and uses it for its own end to distort the truth, to get people to obey. I'm not against organized religion, but spirituality is not religious; spirituality is a way of life. You don't need intermediaries for that.

Again here I must have my say. The next question is a shining example of what Hans truly believes. He clearly states what the ghost business means to him. There are so many individuals across this planet that want to know whether or not a ghost is real. The way Hans describes his theory and belief is astonishing to me. You just can't make that up! Hans truly is still that magical person to me even now as an adult.

LSB: Do you believe in ghosts?

Hans: I don't believe in anything. Belief is the uncritical acceptance of something you can't prove. I work on evidence; I either know or I don't know. There are three dirty words in my vocabulary: belief, disbelief and supernatural. They don't exist. There's no "supernatural world." Everything that exists is natural. Yet there is a dimension of existence that is as real as your living room, even if the average person cannot access it with all their senses? I coined the phrase "the other side" because it really is the other side, like one side of the mirror. The spirit world, or "the world next door," as Eileen Garrett called it, is not up or down. It is here, moving at a different rate of speed. And the dimension into which we all pass — except ghosts, because they can't get into it until they are liberated from their compulsions — is concentric with this dimension. It exists in the same special area, but because it's strung out further, it does not clash with the thicker atmosphere, the thicker dimension, in which we exist.

The next question may leave some of you thinking, well, how would he know? I also pose that question, but I have a deeper understanding and am okay with the possibility of what he is saying is real.

LSB: What's "the other side" like?

Hans: Everything we have here they have over there. It is a duplicate of this world except over there the purpose is to develop the personality from the negative to the positive, or to give them assignments or to send them down for some more education.

Here is also a huge question on many minds as to there being a difference between a spirit and a ghost. Recently when filming for a Californian production company as paranormal experts, we both were asked this question.

LSB: What is the difference between a ghost and a spirit?

Hans: We are all spirit. When we pass on, we simply get rid of the outer layer and, underneath, there really is a duplicate layer. This inner body, like an inner tube of a tire, is where our personality resides. At death the physical body is worn out and dissolved, so the inner body is where we live. So we need to have an atmosphere, a dimension, that fits this inner body and that's the world of spirit, or the etheric world. The etheric world is all around us. At death, we ride out into that world and we are right there. That's our normal transition. However, once in a while something goes wrong when somebody passes from the physical state.

LSB: What turns them into a ghost?

Hans: The death is not smooth. When there is trauma — an unacceptable accident or shock or surprise — this will, in some cases, cause the personality to go into a state of psychotic shock. In that state of shock they are not aware that they've passed on. They are confused as to their real status because they can see everybody and nobody seems to be able to see them. That's what a ghost is... somebody who's gotten stuck in the physical world, but is not part of the physical world. And they become panic stricken for attention and eventually they do things to get attention, like moving objects, creating noises. This is not to frighten people, they're just attention getters.

The next question makes me laugh. Even if the noise we hear in the darkness may not lead to a ghost, most of us tend to think somewhere along those haunting lines. It just seems to be human nature. So much so it becomes a parody in movies where one actor says to another, "Maybe it's a ghost?"

LSB: But not everything that goes bump in the night is a ghost?

Hans: It's the exception rather than the normal transition. I have found that about seventy-five to eighty percent of the sightings or auditory phenomena are not really people stuck in our atmosphere, but replays from the past. Like an imprint on the atmosphere. It's a psychic imprint; an imprint on the atmosphere, which is energy like a television picture that is stuck in time. To the average person it looks exactly the same as a ghost. Even some mediums can't tell the difference. But if phenomena are observed exactly alike at the same time in the same place and a number of witnesses have reported identical experiences, then you probably have an imprint. If, from different witnesses, you have reports saying there's a variation in what the ghost entity is doing, then it's a real person. That's the only way you can tell one from the other.

LSB: How are they different from ghosts who crave attention?

Hans: The ghost personality is generally in various stages of psychotic condition — otherwise they would move on. Those who stay behind is someone who lived in one place for a very long time and usually dies a gentle death; they just fall asleep, no violence, no pain. They are unused to any other place, partially because their religious belief has primed them to believe Hosanna with angels' wings on their back, or in some cases, fellows in red underwear with pitch forks, would take them away. Low and behold, at death, they're still where they were before. The physical body isn't there — but there's a body and they see themselves, so they stay put. That's why people go to the funeral of Aunt Minnie, come back and there she is in her usual chair.

Now here's a good question coming up. Many don't ask this one as it isn't one of the more popular ones. Good question, Reverend!

LSB: You made a distinction between a ghost and a spirit. Is there a distinction between a spirit and a soul?

Hans: No. The soul is the spirit. The soul is the personality. The soul is energy that manifests through and resides in an etheric body. This energy field, which is us, is what the church calls the soul and what the spiritually inclined people call the spirit. Popular culture has offered a few glimpses into the other side. In the movie Ghost, we saw a spirit shocked out of his skin, yet determined to finish some business.

Okay, this next question is a bit silly, however, due to the movie indus-try, it's important to ask. When an audience sees something on the big screen they tend to take it to heart. They're left with an impression that may or may not misguide them in what they just saw. Here in the case of the movie, Ghost, you have a star-studded cast and a plot with the dead coming back. I think it's a good question when seen in that way.

LSB: In your opinion, was the movie *Ghost* an accurate portrayal?

Hans: Everything was correct except for that last scene, which is Holly-wood, where the furries come and get the bad guy. It doesn't work that way. There are no furries, there is no hell. There is only that which you bring with you to the other side. But movies are fantasy. This is real.

Now comes my announcement. I have written a supernatural horror screenplay to do exactly what Hans just said. And I quote my own father, "But movies are fantasy. This is real." My movie must be real as encounter-ing a ghost or anything unknown is scary. By Hans' lifetime career in the ghost business, I was able to pull from my own resources and experiences to have a dream in seeing this movie be real. The fantasy part of it is for the audience, for effect, but for the ghosts, quite real indeed. That would make for an interesting casting call. Ghosts needed for supernatural movie; must be transparent and able to glide well. Back to the article.

LSB: So we do bring our baggage with us at death?

Hans: When you pass on, you take your memories with you. And if your life has been negative or a destructive one, you will have to go to school, so to speak, and the next time around you will have a chance to confront some of those issues again. That's the whole idea behind reincarnation. I did a lot of work on reincarnation for Life Beyond. I have no doubts whatsoever it exists for everybody.

LSB: Yet in between gigs in human form, can our beloved relatives communicate from the other side without being ghosts?

Hans: It's very common. Unfortunately, our culture teaches people that it is not possible... that there is nothing out there. Yet when somebody passes on, the first thing when they arrive on the other side is they want to let their loved ones know that they are still alive and that they are well and they are happy being with other loved ones. There is touching cases where they feel the person. Yes. Oh, all of this is very possible.

Part III

The last of too many worthy articles I am going to introduce is a fairly recent one and I thought it would mix nicely with the previous older ones. This gives you a diverse range in years of Hans and his business of ghosts. It's funny because you'd think he'd call up and tell his family about these interviews, but in short that's not the case. It is quite the opposite in fact. Hans was never about attention or spotlight. He was always humbled and glad to spread the word. What interviews I was able to witness at home were normal and well paced: Catherine sitting on the sofa and Hans around her, chatting away as the words would overflow in the Holzer household. I too, never seem to be at a loss for words. A curse for my husband, but such is life! I'd like to share this final piece as Hans is slowly not doing anymore interviews. He has re-focused back on screenplays and now working with me on radio shows and potentially television again. One never knows where one's path may lead.

In the article, "Dr. Hans Holzer, A Lifetime of Explaining the Unexplained," by Jeff Belanger, Hans, now eighty-five years old, is asked about retirement.

Hans: I retire every day... Every night at midnight.

Reporter: After penning 138 books as well as several plays, musicals, films, and documentaries and hosting a television show, the only thing that slows him down today is a mishap from an operation on his leg three years ago. What does it slow him down from? "Swing dancing," he said. I laughed. Then I realized he wasn't kidding. "Not just swing dancing, any kind of dancing!"

Reporter: Supernaturally speaking, Dr. Holzer has seen and heard it all. He's worked with psychic legends like Sybil Leek, he's investigated some of the most prominent haunted locations around the world, and he's come as close as a living person can to touching the "other side of life" — a term he's quick to point out that he invented. I spoke to Dr. Holzer about his life and work from his office in New York City.

Hans: I have no secrets. I mean, I have secrets, but I don't make them secret. If anybody wants to hear them, they can hear them." .

Next is a bit redundant as you already know by now his year of birth and kindergarten behavior. I sometimes go over that mentally because I just think he was so advanced at his age and often misunderstood. Hans had a gift to entertain and to see things that weren't suppose to be there.

Hans: I was in kindergarten. I was four years old. I see this as vividly today as when it happened. I see myself seated in a little yellow chair with all of the other kids around, and I was in the middle, pretending to read from an expired streetcar pass of my father's. I couldn't read at four, but I pretended. And I was 'reading' them ghost stories. Obviously fictional ghost stories, but the kids loved it. The only trouble was that they told their parents at home.

The next thing that happened was the mothers came in and said, 'What kind of a kindergarten are we running here?' And so my mother was brought in, and the teacher said, 'Look, either he goes or I go.' At that point, I stopped telling ghost stories.

Reporter: What was your first paranormal experience?

Hans: It's not a question of whether I had experiences. My interest has nothing to do with personal experiences. In other words, you don't have to be an investigator to experience things first-hand.

Reporter: For Holzer, each case must with stand journalistic integrity, and journalism is just one of the many subjects he studied during his academic career.

Hans: I took ancient history and archaeology at the University of Vienna. Then I spent another three and a half years at Columbia University where I studied Japanese. In addition, I was a graduate of the Academy of Journalism in Vienna, which was a total waste of time. But I took it — it sounded nice. At the end, I studied at the London College of Applied Science, which awarded me a master's in comparative religion, and then a year later, a Ph.D. with a specialty in parapsychology.

Reporter: I've read you don't like the term 'supernatural.'

Hans: I use the term because it is the one that people use, but nothing in my scientific view does not have an explanation. The question is, sooner we get it or later we get it, but there has to be an explanation. You can't say nobody knows. I don't accept that. And the paranormal is part of our experience, we just don't always understand it as such. That's why I want to know my witness. 'Who are you? What do you do for a living?' I interview the witnesses. If there is a crazy in front of me, I'll know it.

Hans is asked a similar question from the interview in Part II and his response is even better this time around. Sometimes we speak more in-depth when asked repeatedly over a course of time. I think it's pretty neat.

Hans: My first visual experience was when I lived in New York City with my father in a penthouse apartment on Riverside Drive. I was asleep in bed, and I woke up and there was my mother dressed in a white nightgown, pushing my head back onto the pillow. My head had slipped off the pillow. At that time I was subject to migraines. Had I not had my head back on the pillow, I probably would've had one, and there would've been dizziness and I would've been out of business for a day. I said, 'Oh, hello, Mama.' And she disappeared.

Reporter: We talked about the difference between a ghost or a spirit, how a ghost is a residual entity, like a psychic imprint left in an area that some people can pick up, whereas a spirit is intelligent and interactive. Holzer also mentioned a third category I hadn't heard about before: the "stay behinds."

See, something new is learned after all of Hans' years in the biz. Hans never grows tired of being asked the same questions over and over again. He loves it and for over six decades could just as easily pushed it all off saying, 'enough!' But Hans never did and never will. You gotta admire him after all, many in the spotlight tend to do their interviews with a thank you, have a nice day, now go away. Not Hans Holzer. A true professional time and time and decade again.

Hans: 'Stay behinds' are relatively common… Somebody dies, and then they're really surprised that all of a sudden they're not dead. They're alive like they were. They don't understand it because they weren't prepared for it. So they go back to what they knew most, their chair, their room, and they just sit there. Next, they want to let people know that they're still 'alive.' So they'll do little things like moving things, appear to relatives, pushing objects, poltergeist phenomena, and so on.

Reporter: Preparation for the after life is something most world religions devote their very existence to. Holzer believes all religions have some of it right in that they believe in a supreme power, a belief Holzer also holds. He considers himself an Evangelical Protestant and used to attend St. Bartholomew in Manhattan twice a year — on Christmas and Easter. But he has since stopped going as he's been at odds with the minister. I asked him why.

Hans: They were running a seminar on world religions, they had a Rabbi there, they had an Imam there, it was a discussion group. Since I'm a professional lecturer, I offered to add the view of parapsychology. And he [the minister] turned it down with a note saying, 'How can you compare that with what we're doing?' And I didn't think that was very nice. You have to understand where I'm coming from, if it weren't for parapsychology, religion wouldn't have a leg to stand on because they have used what we call the facts of the paranormal to build their messages of faith. Religion works on faith and on belief and disbelief, you must do this and you must do that, that's not where science comes from. Science gives the facts whether you like them or not, and you have to accept them or not accept them, but it's not a question of belief or faith.

Here Hans begins to show his furthered interest in the scientific view and religion. His path was beginning to change its course and I didn't even recognize this until he sent me his latest book on the topic. Hans is like that. He goes about his business and you're always the last to know. But, when you do know, you have lots of questions to ask, which makes him a great writer and thinker of our times.

Hans: I am working on early Christianity as part of the research work, and I have come up with some very startling facts about early Christianity that differ markedly from what the Roman Catholic and even my own church are convinced of. And while I'm working on this, I would feel like a fool going to church. For instance, I spent fifteen years of research establishing that Jesus Christ, that is Jeshua, was born October the third, seven B.C., beyond the shadow of a doubt. We have the hard evidence from contemporary sources. So how could I possibly go and celebrate Christmas? The church at the Council of Nicea in 325, since they weren't sure when Jesus was born either, decided to make it officially on a day which was already a holiday, this was Saturnalia of the Roman calendar, the 25th of December. October the third is the correct date. I wrote a book about this called *A Star in the East*.

Reporter: Though the date might be wrong, is the message right?

Hans: I'm not condemning all religions... I'm condemning certain portions of it as being man-made and used solely for selfish purposes. There are some wonderful concepts in religion; Buddhism has a lot of good things, for instance.

I think that spirituality is a personal thing unique to you. It doesn't cost anything and it doesn't take any effort. We should all have a spiritual concept of life.

Reporter: I asked him what we can expect to find waiting for us on the other side.

Hans: We all pass out of the physical body and we are now on the other side of life. It's a world just like this one, it has only two differences: there's no sense of time, and if you're ill when you die, you're now no longer ill. But other than that, you'll find houses, trees, gardens, and your relatives, friends, and so on. It looks like a very real world. Maybe a little nicer, but still a normal, real world. And you are just the way you were before. Maybe a little bit younger looking if you wish, but you're still in a very real world.

Isn't it lovely to think that when we cross over it can be this way? What is the harm of Hans' beliefs if it can lead us to good lives and we can go to a place like that? I say, "Here, here," to that, Hans. I can think of worse things to think about, especially these days in a time of war and change. On with the article.

Hans: You'll notice that the other side of life is a bureaucracy just like this one. You can't just call Uncle Frank [who's still living]. You have to get permission from a group of people who call themselves guides, spirit guides. They will say, 'Why do you want to make contact? What's your purpose?' And if they approve of it, they'll say, 'Okay, find yourself a medium somewhere, speak with them, and they will make contact for you.' Or if you're that strong, you can try to make contact yourself. And if you don't like where you are after awhile, you may have a consciousness that you've been there a certain period and feel that you would rather be back on the other side with friends and loved ones. You'll say, 'I'd like to get reborn again.' These are the words I got from them, they're not my invention. They [the spirits] said you have to go to a line, and you have to register with the clerk. 'Clerk' is the word they used. So you get in line and register with the clerk that you want to go back. The clerk says, 'Okay, I'll let you know when I find an appropriate couple for you that will advance your development.' They have no real sense of time, so they just stand there, and eventually the clerk will say, 'I've got a couple for you.' There is a well and they [the spirit about to go back] must walk through that well. They call it, 'The Well of Forgetfulness.' They are sprayed with this water, not 100 percent, it never quite covers everything. That's why people have memories, dejá vu experiences, and recurrent dreams. And then they are a baby again.

I love how Hans uses the word 'clerk.' He still does whenever we have a discussion on the afterlife and my experiences.

Hans: What I have learned in my investigations is that there are seven levels of consciousness on the other side of life that are concentric with our world. It's not up or down, it's just concentric. We can't see it because it moves at a different rate of speed than we move. There's three levels when you are born. You are born with a physical outer body, a duplicate inner body, and at the very moment of birth, that's very important, the moment the child is supposed to see the light [during childbirth], that is when the soul or the spirit is inserted from the pool of available spirits from the other side. Therefore, all this nonsense about abortion killing a child is pure lies, pure nonsense. The fetus, until the spirit of the child is inserted, is a physical part of the mother. It does not have any life — it's not a separate entity.

This could get Hans into hot water. Especially being a woman myself with four children, I could even take it a certain way. Parent or not, I too will disagree even with the master of ghosts. In any case, I will not touch the last statement Hans makes with a ten foot pole! Onward and forward.

Reporter: Holzer said he worked with several mediums to compile this information on how things work in the afterlife. Holzer believes a good medium is the most critical element to a good supernatural investigation. He believes the medium is the person who can speak for those on the other side and deliver clear messages. "That's putting a lot of faith in a person who is hopefully not a charlatan, but could be," I said.

Hans: That's why you don't ask questions of a psychic. You just sit there and listen. I'll give you an example. Philip Solomon, a British trance medium, once called me out of the blue because I had written a rather harsh piece in a magazine. It was about psychics who didn't deliver, not fakers, but incompetent psychics. So we talked on the phone and became friendly, and then he suddenly said, 'Your uncle Henry is here.' It became clear that he was talking about somebody who really is my uncle Henry. Weeks went on, and from time to time, he would call me and give me messages from my parents and from Henry, which I found valid. Months went by, and he [Philip Solomon] said, 'Yes, Uncle Henry is here again.' So I said, 'If it's my uncle Henry, what does he want me to know?' And Philip said, 'Just a moment.' And then he came back and said, 'Your uncle Henry says the dog's name was Rigo.' Who the hell would know that? But it was Rigo. That's what I call evidence. There was no way that he could have known that my uncle's dog's name was Rigo. No way he could have known that, that was years and years ago. The only explanation of that particular case was that this was my uncle Henry. That was his way of proving himself. That's the kind of evidence I demand. It cannot be explained away.

Hans: We are living in a technological age and they [paranormal investigators] think, or at least some of them that I've met, in all sincerity, that running around with geiger counters and cameras and instruments that can measure cold spots will be the way to investigate a haunting or a ghost. That's bullshit. Because if you really are an investigator of the paranormal, and you're dealing with ghosts or haunting's, you're dealing with a human being — nothing more, nothing less. Therefore you should have with you a good trance medium who can lend her body or his body temporarily for that entity to speak through so you can find out what the trouble is. That's the way it works, not a geiger counter.

Reporter: But certainly a geiger counter is more accessible than a good trance medium for most people.

Hans: And it looks more professional to them, but it really is bullshit... I have worked with psychic photographers — that's a special form of mediumship. Psychic photography is a gift. Some have it. I've used these people in haunted places. When there was something there, they would photograph it.

Reporter: Have you ever been afraid during an investigation?

Hans: Fear is the absence of information, fear is created by not understanding something. You bring on the fear. There is no object to fear. I've never been afraid during an investigation. I shouldn't be in this business if I was.

Okay. At this part I have to talk about my orbs. Not 'those' kind of orbs for some of you thinking another way. When I began to tune into my abilities after my late Aunt Rosemarie came back pushing me to write, something began happening to my picture taking. I was getting 'anomalies,' as they call it, and I was so excited at this discovery. I rushed to the phone to call Hans and I got the typical Hans reaction. I said to myself, "Here comes the Holzerisms." He says to me, "Yes, and so what else is new? How are the kids?" I was confused and thought I had embarked on something great. He then hears the defining silence on the other end of the phone and asks the question again. So, I responded, but went back to the main reason of the phone call. "So, I am getting these orbs on my pictures and not just at home. Wherever I go, there they are."

"Well, then you are attracting energy and those around you from the other side," said Hans.

I couldn't wait to show them to him the next time I saw him! The next month we went to my sister's house for a get-together. When the Holzers do this, it always includes both Catherine and Hans even after all this time. Isn't that great? For my sister and I and our children, it is a beautiful thing. In any case, we were in Riverdale, New York at her apartment and I bust out my photos. I'm showing my sister, mother, the cat... and then I sit beside Hans. "Okay, dad. Here they are — the pictures I told you about. The orbs?" After he looks for his glasses, which are already on his face, he takes hold of photo number one. He looks at it, turns away from it and back in again. He grunts, sniffles, and then speaks. "I can't tell what this is," he said. Annoyed I pointed out the obvious. He looks again and still disagrees. So, I decide to show him a face that both Catherine and I were emailing one another back and forth seeing the exact same impression. Hans looks at the second photo and does the same thing. Now I'm getting a bit pissy and feel I need to explain what has been going on. Uh oh! Big mistake.

Hans looks at me and says, "Look, I don't see it and I don't believe that is a ghost. Perhaps energy yes, but I don't see a face!" My sister, to the rescue, chimes in after looking at the same photo. "Look dad, see I can see it too." The photo was actually taken at my sister's the last time we visited. A ghostly apparition in an orb formation appeared behind her as she was in the photo. So, what was I going to do? Argue with the master? You bet! He seems to forget I am his daughter and can have just as sharp if not sharper tongue. The next ten minutes would evolve into a heated debate between my father and I. In the end, we both agreed to disagree and left it at that. I lunged at my glass of wine while the children ran amuck. Life is not perfect and even those who are experts on something sometimes don't know everything! However, I respected him and gave him the last word, which was difficult to do. I knew he believed in taking pictures of the dead, just not orbs in general.

For him he must see the whole enchilada, not just a floating circular glob. But I did have faces and sometimes figures as my pictures became more advanced. After awhile I stopped taking them all together. What was the point. I knew they existed and was satisfied with that.

Hans: There's nothing out there that isn't one way or the other human. Hollywood not withstanding, there are no monsters out there. There is no other supernatural race, no devils, no fellows in red underwear. It doesn't exist.

Reporter: What have you learned about yourself during all of these years of investigations?

Hans: My purpose is that I have a job. First of all, the other side, being a bureaucracy and being a well-ordered world, invests in people's abilities. When the other side decides some individuals have very good minds and good hearts, then they are given talents with the proviso that they will use those talents for the betterment of the world and mankind. If you don't, they won't like it. So they make it very plain: you have a gift. Use it. I found out early enough that they had something in mind for me. I accepted that it's an assignment. I noticed that what happened to me was kind of programmed. I met some people who were important for my career, or for my enlightenment, it was all arranged. So I finally said, 'Friends, I noticed you're running my life. It's okay with me. I will do it.' And I hear this in my right ear: 'We will guide you, help you. Use your gifts. You have two separate paths, one has to do with science, parapsychology research, and the other has to be the entertainment business. But you combine them to let the world know what you find.' And that's what I do.

Hans (on being a vegan): It makes a difference. You may not like to hear this, but it does make a difference. The last cold I had was fifteen years ago. I don't take injections of any kind or prescription drugs. And I intend to be around a long time.

Reporter: Do you have any vices at all?

Hans: Sure! I love to chase women, but chasing and catching them you know are two different things. I have many women friends and I have few men friends. That's not my fault; it seems to be the way it is. Because women are much more sensitive to the psychic world. But I have many friends.

Can I tell you he had more statues and paintings in the house of women's breasts than I thought was normal. Especially in his office. When you walked into that office, it was like a shrine to the dead. That's coming up in a later chapter.

Hans: I have a lot to do that needs to be done. A lot of it is not yet finished. I think retirement is a terrible mistake... People can be unhappy for two reasons: because they have the wrong mate or because they have the wrong job. They can change both.

Reporter: How do you want to be remembered?

Okay, here is where I believe this memoir is fitting. Hans would have never thought one of his children would carry on his legacy and continue on the Holzer name in the publishing industry. And as an added bonus, carrying on the interest in the paranormal. It is interesting to hear what his answer was.

Hans: As a man who told the truth. I won't have a tombstone. Cemeteries are real estate wastes, and I don't believe in funerals of any kind. The sooner you burn the body the better. It's just a shell. Mankind has a lot to learn. I'm particularly concerned about mankind's continuing preoccupation with violence, war, and crime. I think one of the problems with our generations is that there is no spirituality. And what I'm sort of selling, if you wish; instead of religion, which means to re-link with the deity, really, I sell something called the spiritual way of life. That is to say, instead of going to church at 11 on Sunday once a week, you live it seven days a week, twenty-four hours a day. Your conduct is spiritual no matter what you do; you follow a spiritual, moral concept. And that's all you should do. Just live it.

Reporter: What will you be doing on your 100th birthday?

I would think still looking for his glasses and camera!

Hans: Looking forward to my 101st... I do what I'm meant to do. A man who takes himself too seriously, others won't take seriously, so I'm very careful about that. I want to be factual and to be useful and I try to help anybody who wants help.

Reporter: And you want to keep swing dancing?

Hans: Yes... Not just swing, any form of dancing. When my (older) daughter saw me at the wedding of my younger daughter, [she] saw all of us on the dance floor and said, 'I didn't know you had in you, Daddy.' I said, 'What do you think I do, the Govotte?'

Yes, my wedding... with that blue tux, velvet collar and black bow tie...lovely. But he had moves... he had moves. I remember when he used to get passes to a club in the city called 'The Limelight' and would tell me to go have fun. I went once and never again. It was in a church for crying out loud! "Are you nuts?" I said to Hans one evening. "Yes!" and with that, he walked back into his office.

Reporter: "Dr. Hans Holzer has two daughters and five grandchildren. He was married once, but divorced after the birth of his second daughter. He's committed to explaining the unexplained, to living a spiritual life, and to dancing. In Joseph Campbell's book, *Myths to Live By*, he describes a conference on religion that took place in Japan. A social philosopher approaches a Japanese Shinto Priest and says, 'We've been now to a good many ceremonies and have seen quite a few of your shrines. But I don't get your ideology. I don't get your theology.' The Priest thinks about this for a moment and then responds, 'I think we don't have ideology. We don't have theology. We dance.' Thanks for dancing with me, Dr. Holzer.

Chapter Seventeen:

HANS' LAIR

I mentioned in last chapter Hans' office. I refer to it as his "lair" because as a child it seemed to be something out of Dungeons and Dragons. Bear in mind, what a child sees versus an adult are two completely different versions. That's why I enjoy writing fantasy and science fiction. It brings me back to the mind of a child and how fabulous is that. Entering Hans' lair always began with a slight knocking at his half ajar door. Sometimes he'd answer with a forceful "yes!" and other times a softer "come in," but either way he answered, it was always proper to knock beforehand. After all, he could be in there stirring up a witches' brew or casting some sort of spell. Gently pushing the door open, my little feet prodded in on the oriental runner leading to his squeaky chair. He'd only have his desk lamp on, which I surmise now is the reason for why his lenses have thickened. Funny, even now as I am typing, I too just have my desk lamp on. Like father, like daughter I suppose. Without looking up — he'd be typing away on his powder blue Smith Corona — he'd inquire, "Yes, what is it?" Sometimes I'd go in to tell him a trivial thing and other times just to let him know if I was in need of something. But, mainly just to sit on his brown psychiatrist style couch and watch him work. I'd look around the long thin office as I did a hundred times before. Up on his wall was my favorite place to start....

Framed in black he'd have pictures of Tina Louise and other actresses showing their bosoms. Then, on an odd angle he'd have framed signatures. They were scribbled so tightly that one could mistaken it for a doctor's note. After the wall, I'd peer out the window, then off to one of his bookcases. Riddled with his titles from left to right, he'd have little knick-knacks on the bookshelves themselves. Some were glass bottles with labels on them: Eye of Nut, Frogs Nails, Witch Hazel and on it went. Mixed in with that were bizarre stuffed objects that friends of his would give to him over time. He had a cackling witch that when you smacked her bottom, she made this horrible laughing sound. Other toys would be demonic looking cats and, by the way, we had that black cat, so that theory went out the window. I used to pretend she was a witch. We named her Sylvia. Hans took me to get her to replace my guinea pig. He always believed in going to the shelters and never buying an animal because there were so many in need of a home. One time I came home with a mom cat and her two babies, and Hans let me keep them until we found a good home. It disrupted Sylvia's home front, but it was for a good cause. Hans panicked over Sylvia's behavior, but I took care of everything so that he could be at peace with the rescue mission.

Adjacent to the wall with the smaller bookcase was a larger, longer wall. Here was the more prominent book case and more of his titles just pouring out of the office. Above the bookcase, he had nails in the wall holding necklaces and other gothic items. It was a bizarre display, but what was comfortable for him. The bottles of colored liquids I dared not go near. One time, he had a woman who said she was a witch come over and they disappeared into his "lair." I wondered whether or not a black caldron was taken out from beneath his couch and used for some sort of ritual. I used to say to myself that if he ever did that, I would hope he'd do a spell to give himself more hair.

There was also a unique aroma that went with this office. A hint of cologne, flowers and incense all mixed together. Hans loved his incense boat. Sometimes he even took it out of his office and placed it on the living room bookcase shelves. Catherine enjoyed it as well. It kind of gave a mystical feel to the apartment late at night and let my mind to wander yet again.

Hans' office was the center of all his writing and creations. It was the brain of the operations. Inside that office, magic happened into the wee hours of the night.

One of my fondest memories was hearing him type away until 2 a.m. It was my lullaby at bedtime. Forget story time, I just needed to hear those tapping keys and I was off to slumber land. Of course my slumber land was filled with witches, ghosts and beds flying through the night sky. In fact one of my favorite books was "Bed knobs and Broomsticks," partly due to Hans' influence in the house. Hans fed my imagination and layered it with years and years of great material. Catherine laced my mind with beautiful colors and swirls of the paintbrush. Growing up in that house made me dizzy at times. Not to mention the mere fact that I had an occasional ghost or two sit on me or pass my way. I could sit here and go through every accomplishment that Hans ever made, but that would miss the point. He was born into this world ready for action. I feel the same for myself. If we're not moving and shaking, then we're not happy and that is a Holzer.

The heart of Hans' office was his closet. Inside this closet he kept all his movie reels with black negative tape strewn about. The tape would hang over bundles of screenplays and folders filled with manuscripts to the hilt. If a fire ever caught in there, it could heat up the entire building for a year! Hans wasn't the neatest of neat, but he had his way. Everything in its place and a place for everything, he would say. If I even approached that closet, he'd be quick to move me in another direction. When I was a teenager, it got so full that once he had to remove the closet door all together. There it was out in the open for all to see — a lifetime of work, bursting at its seams. I respected the work pile nonetheless, and from time to time would look on admirably at it wondering what the heck it all said. In that office there'd be a story for everything.

One time, during one of my sittings, he began to tell me of a time way back when. One of my favorites was his story about Brigadoon. It was sheer and utter magic. It started off when he was a young lad visiting Ireland. There was a place called Brigadoon that was said to vanish before the townspeople's eyes. He claimed he was there at a local pub. I thought this odd being Hans was never much of a drinker, but then again, he went everywhere for a story of the unknown so why not a local pub. He said it was late one evening, dank and foggy… just as I pictured Ireland to be. He left the pub and wandered off to a tree to rest awhile. There he heard a tiny little voice. As he peered down, there was a little man speaking to him. Hans couldn't quite make out what was being said to him, but rubbed his eyes many times. Not thrilled with what he just experienced, he left the premise at once. Off in the distance he thought he saw a town. As he was on foot, curiously approaching it, it vanished as quickly as it had appeared mere moments ago. I loved this story and, whether it was true or not didn't matter. It was great and I took it with me, and created a world of my own to imagine all sorts of things; pots of gold, Leprechauns, invisible towns, and more. Then I saw the movie with Gene Kelly, 'Brigadoon,' and I completely fell in love with the story all over again.

One thing Hans could do was tell a great mysterious and wondrous story. Through Hans, my eyes grew larger each day. My thoughts expanded to unknown horizons and untouched places. Catherine showered those places with illuminating tones and vivid colors, giving way to one far out mind. That office was a safe haven for me at times during New York City thunderstorms. I say New York thunderstorms because back then, when they hit the Hudson

River, it was like entities were surging into the water and coming alive. The water would turn from black to grey and bubble over. High winds would pick up speed and toss the tall Riverside Park trees around like salad. Cars down below seemed to slow down as the lights stopped changing. The entire park stood still as the river's edge rose. The only place that I could escape the thunderous sound of those storms was in that office bathroom. Off I went when Catherine tapped me to go and I'd slam that door behind me. I didn't care that I got a few strands of hair caught, just as long as I didn't hear that awful searing noise. Some kids are told to count in between the lightning to see the storm is moving away. Not me. I just ran and hid until it was over. Who needed counting! And it didn't even work for that kid in the film, *Poltergeist,* so the heck with that! I had Hans' lair to protect me and that was fine by me.

Chapter Eighteen:

Hans is on the Case

Although you can purchase any one of the many books on the investigative work Hans conducted over the years, I felt it necessary to include some of his favorites famous ghost stories that he personally shared with Nadine and I growing up. This later was placed into a book Hans wrote as a "Haunted Travel Guide" by Black Dog and Leventhal Publishers in New York.

Case No. 1-NYC Law School: The Dorm with a Ghostly Past

As Hans begins, "until a few years ago, the Cafe Bizarre (a cafe and bar) could be found on the corner of 3rd Street and Sullivan. Before it was a cafe, the building was part of Aaron Burr's private stables, and on a few separate occasions, the ghost of Aaron Burr, has been spotted in and around the cafe. A young woman named Alice McDermott was having a drink with some friends one night — she looked up from her conversation and saw a strange man, dressed in the eighteenth century style clothing peering at her from the balcony above. Her account is consistent with those of Rick Allmen, the former owner of the cafe. Subsequently, I conducted a seance with the help of medium Sybil Leek and Burr's ghost spoke through her. He complained bitterly about the injustices of history on his reputation, lamented his exile to France, and spoke of his daughter Theodosia, who died in a storm at sea. It was clear that the former Vice President had no intention of leaving his stable. Later on the building was razed, and a much larger building was erected on the site. Today, The D'Agostino Residence Hall, which is part of NYU Law School, is still the home of the ghost of Aaron Burr. A ghost, unless exorcised from its place, will remain attached to the physical space."

Case No. 2-The Ghost in the Bar: Il Brunello

"There is an Italian Restaurant on West 56th Street, near Sixth Avenue, Il Brunello: a fairly typical little Italian bistro. Many years ago, however, it was a bar called Davinci's, where many a midtown executive would go to unwind with a drink after a long day at work. It was during that period, in the 1950s, when a particular advertising executive, who was a frequent guest at the bar, took to drinking regularly and heavily. Eventually, the Davinci bar become his home away from home, and there were more than a few times that the bartender had to cut him off because he had simply had a few too many. When he died, he apparently never quite left his favorite bar and hang out. Soon after his death, the bartenders would spot glasses on the bar half filled with Martinis, after the bar had been shut tight for the night. Advertising slogans appeared mysteriously on the wall when no one was in the place. I held a seance there with the late medium Ethel Johnson Meyers, to try to persuade the advertising man to leave for a better place: which he refused to do, but when the medium came out of deep trance, she was visibly drunk!"

Case No. 3-Poughkeepsie, New York at the Church of Christ Rectory

"Bishop James Pike, one time Bishop of California and the author of a number of remarkable books, was no stranger to psychic phenomena. During my work with him, he got to know the Church Rectory at Poughkeepsie pretty well. In 1947, Pike was offered the position of Rector, and spent several years there. The Church of Christ is a large, beautiful, Episcopal Church. The altar is somewhat "high church" that is similar to Roman Catholic style. The church exterior and attached rectory remain turn-of-the-century. There is also a small library between the rectory and the church. What occurred during the two and a half years of Pike's residency at Poughkeepsie was not unusual, as hauntings go. To him, it was merely puzzling and he made no attempt to follow up on it as I did when he brought a medium to the scene. Pike had taken over his position at Poughkeepsie, replacing an elderly rector with diametrically opposed views in church matters. The former rector had died shortly afterward. Pike sound found that his altar candles were being blown out, doors shut of their own volition, and objects over head would move – or seem to – when in fact they did not. All the noises and disturbances did not particularly upset Bishop Pike. However, on one occasion he found himself faced with a bat flying madly about in the library. Knowing that there was no way in or out of the library except by the door he had just opened, he immediately closed the door again and went to look for an instrument for which to capture the bat. When he returned and cautiously opened the door to the library, the bat disappeared."

Case No. 4-The Ghosts at Gettysburg

"Gettysburg, Pennsylvania is the site of one of the most significant battles of the Civil War, and later, of Lincoln's infamous address. At one point in his speech, President Lincoln said that, "these dead shall not have died in vain," an interesting prelude to the ghosts that continue to haunt the battlefield. On the battlefield, there is a spot called Little Round Top, where one of the bloodiest engagements of the war took place. Today, you will find a historical monument and memorials to the soldiers who died there. There have been a number of sightings of a phantom soldier wandering this area — he appears to be looking for his regiment and is clearly not cognizant that he has been killed in battle. Another ghostly tale in this area takes place in an old Inn called Graeffenburg, which stands next to the battlefield. A young woman named Helen Forrest was born there, and her family ran the small tourist hotel. Even as a young girl, Helen recalls hearing a woman's voice in her room when no one was there. The ghost would sing, open windows, move furniture, and leave a faint Lilac scent in room 32. Helen's father refused to let anyone stay in that room — a tradition that has, for the most part, continued to this day, even though Mr. Forrest has long since passed. Helen returned to the Inn when she was in her thirties and requested room 32 for the night. The manager told her that two of the previous managers had stayed in the room, and both were smothered to death while they slept. Helen decided to stay in the room anyway. In the middle of the night, she awakened from a deep sleep, to find herself being shaken violently awake. She leapt out of bed to find the room ablaze and a small old woman in a nightgown gazing at her and standing amidst the flames. The room was gutted, but since restored and open to visitors."

Case No. 5-Ringwood Manor, New Jersey

"One of the most interesting haunted houses I have visited is only an hour's drive from me. It is a manor house known locally as Ringwood Manor, and is considered one of the more important historical houses in New Jersey. Built on land purchased by the Ogden family in 1740, it originally was the home of the owners of a successful iron-smelting furnace. In 1936, Erskine Hewitt left the estate to the state of New Jersey, and the mansion is now a museum. Not too many visitors come, however, since Ringwood Manor does not get the kind of attention some of the better publicized national shrines attract. I visited the manor with the late Ethel Johnson-Myers to follow up on persistent reports of hauntings in the old mansion. One of the chief witnesses to the ghostly activities was the manor superintendent. He had heard footsteps when no one was around — footsteps of two different people. Doors that have been shut at night were wide open in the morning, yet no one had been around yet to open them. The feeling of "presences" in various parts of the house persisted. A local legend says that the ghost of Robert Erskine, the owner of the manor and the iron-making operation during the Revolutionary War, walks about with a lantern, but there is no evidence to substantiate this legend. The center of the hauntings is in the bedroom areas, but also along the corridors upstairs and downstairs are spots where a sensitive person might experience chills or cold, clammy feelings. I made contact with the surviving personality of Mrs. Erskine, as well as an unhappy servant named Jeremiah. The manor is a museum and the guides are not shy about talking about the ghosts there."

Later on, I, visited the site and experienced many cold spots during the summer months when the visit took place. The house was too old to renovate to place air conditioning. So, when you went upstairs, it become warmer and a bit claustrophobic as the corridors are very narrow. The rooms are roped off, so I placed my hand over the velvet rope to feel. When I placed my arm inside one of the bedrooms, presumably Mrs. Erskines', it was freezing cold and soon I became dizzy. When I quickly took away my arm, I warmed up and just wanted to keep on moving. All the time feeling as if a female presence, in a long period reddish maroon gown with a swirl like imprint, with her hair up looking sideways, was noticing me. At this time, I was younger and not in appreciation of ghostly impressions left behind and so couldn't tap into it much. But, I am a sensitive individual which makes for one spooky recipe for detecting the unknown!

Chapter Nineteen:

CATHERINE'S TURN

Interesting Fact Finding Lineage

will say one thing on the topic of Catherine the Great and then there is no reason to go further. There is much written on her and her family, so I will explain the great connection. Catherine the Great's daughter, Natalie, married a Buxhoeveden, and so began the lineage of the relations to the Greats. Later on in the book, you will read about an amazing history and private letters during the war in which some characters will be explained in greater detail. Real princesses, Imperial families and Counts, but next up for discussion is a re-cap of the Buxhoevedens and some lineage with great history behind it....

The Buxhoeveden family dates back to the ninth century in the 800s. The Baron's split up the family. In 1201, as you now know, the Buxhoevedens founded a town called Riga in Astonia. There they settled as land owners. Many Buxhoevedens went on to become bishops and generals, winning medals from the war. Grandfather was born in St. Petersburg, Russia. His first marriage yielded five children; out of the five, three passed during World War I. In 1917, there was the Revolution named White Russians, which were the nobilities at the time. The national language spoken then was French. Grandfather's brother had escaped to Helsinki, Finland during the war, and so the battle for survival began as children were born and war took over the borders, leaving many without a country. *Horrible times — I can't even begin to imagine what they were feeling inside while on the outside staying strong for the family.*

The beginning of the timeline is meant to describe the incredible changes to the Buxhoeveden family up to where my grandfather comes into the picture and thereafter. It is a nostalgic and important piece of history. Who was the Russian Count they called Sacha? Born in St. Petersburg in the time of Old Russia, he spent his childhood mainly in the Chateau Laude in Estonia. He went to law school although preferring a career in the military, obeying his parents wishes. Marrying very young to a beautiful widow, he was cut off from his family in disapproval of the marriage. He began a family of his own. With the aid of his wife's family, he bought property and farmed it. He loved the country life and developed the land, adding livestock. Rising every morning he ran this enormous domain in Russia. There his children were born and raised. His son was named Anatole with three girls, twins Elizabeth and Olga, and Mika, the youngest. He had another daughter, but she died at an early age. His life was interrupted when he was named adjutant to the military government in Moscow. The revolution had already been going on for sometime. He was very much in fear as the lives of important people were threatened by car bombs. He succeeded against these attempts, but the Czar and his government were too weak to take the necessary measures. The Count witnessed one of his friends, a journalist, being killed beside him. With his audacious character and patriotic nature, he organized a group of young men to counter the revolutionaries. That made him enemies even in Court, so he left to spend time abroad. Upon his return, he went to his land in Tamboff.

The war broke out in 1914 and he became a volunteer with the regiment of cossacks. The revolution began in 1917, after which the Bolsheviks took power and Lenin made peace with Germany. Count Alexander foresaw what would happen and sent his parents and the family of his brother in Finland away. He sent his daughters with their governess to France. The Countess left for Sweden with their son Anatole. The Count, alone now, returned to St. Petersburg, then Moscow, always in the cossack uniform trying to save those from the bloody rampage of the Bolsheviks. His property had been confiscated and he lived in a hotel in town. One day some marines stopped him. He carried on him a sum of money in rubles and hid it in his shoe. He was led far away to a deserted spot, locked in a room with his money and gun taken away. He was betrayed. He was told that he would be interrogated the next day by a commissar of the people. Throughout the night, he heard them in lively discussion and they decided to free him. They made him sign a piece of paper that his money had been rendered. They didn't give back the gun. Sacha protested, understanding their trap. "How can I return so far in the night without protection?" he asked. They smiled and told him to leave. He hadn't taken more than ten steps onto the road when two marines put their revolvers to his temples. "Give us your money or we pull the trigger." But they set him free after being told what happened and the paper he had signed. He returned on foot back to the capital thinking that this money saved him for the time being. The marines, believing his honesty, knew that as well. Nevertheless, the next time was more grave. He was thrown into a room with other prisoners and was unable to move or lie down.

Each morning the jailers came to the call the prisoners' names. They led some into a courtyard and shot them under the windows and left the corpses till the next day when it would begin again. The Count was saved by the intervention of the German government that his wife and friends begged to intervene. The ambassador insisted that the Buxhoevedens came from Estonia being of Baltic nobility and thus subject to German origin. For this, he was released and received exile from the embassy, but it wasn't without the demand that he leave Russia immediately. This would be the only time he could be saved. Alexander would recount that when he was interrogated during his arrests, he gave his name clearly because many times prisoners were so fearful, hiding their titles. At the next interrogation, the commissar said to him, "Come here, count." A strong character impressed them more than fear.

After having been freed, he rejoined the white Army that fought against the revolutionaries to try and free the Imperial family. An army was commanded under General Wangel, the other, by General Youdenisth. Alexander was in charge of forming the new government if they retook power. He certainly would have been capable of forming a government more democratic, a coalition of all the parties despite the fact that his ideas were monarchistic. He also had a safe conduct pass that allowed him to move between Allied lines. Germany refused to give aid, partly due to having Lenin in Russia. In France, the aid was received by Clemenceau called the Tiger, who held very socialistic opinions and wanted to do nothing against the revolutionaries. Even against the interests of France and the French, who had loaned money to Czarist Russia and then the Bolsheviks, not recognizing the debt. The English appeared to be more sympathetic to the cause of the Whites. They received arms and munitions and a British battleship that came to bombard a fort attacked by Youdenitch. Unfortunately, the Admiral forced the Russians to attack when they were not ready, the ammunition was not with the weapons, the English canons didn't fall on the fort...what sort of treachery? Alas, the White Army lost the struggle.

Alexander found refuge first in Stockholm, where he rejoined a part of his family. At the same hotel was the famous banker of the Czar, Rubenstein and his family. It was believed that Alexander had helped this man as he did others, but made very little mention of it. For the family Buxhoeveden, it was then to Wiesbaden, where he could buy a pretty villa at a good price due to the declining of the Marc. After selling it and making a profit, they came to France. First Paris, where Alexander bought the mansion of Prince Karatgeorvitch of Serbia located on the Bois de Bologne. They lived there for some time as Alexander had the idea to transform it into apartments and sell them. He then went to Nice and began purchasing land for constructing modern buildings; one in Nice, one at Juan Les Pins, one at Beau Soleil, and finally, one at Cannes sur la Croisett. He lived separated from his wife for a long time, not wanting a divorce due to the children. They eventually did divorce in Nice. He then bought a villa in which he and his future wife, Rosine Claire Vidal, would live in at Cimiez. It had been constructed for the Crown Prince of Belgium.

The Buxhoevedens dating as far back in Bavaria to 1184 later were the Barons living in Estonia, but were still subjects of Russia. General Van Frederik Buxhoeveden was named Count by Catherine the Great, then married the daughter of Count Orlof, Nathalia. He was then named the Viceroy of Poland and fought Napoleon's troops many times and was beaten often by them. Nonetheless, the line of Counts began…

· **Paris, April 27, 1927**: Princess Vera Meshchersky founded the 'Russian House' in the Rue de la Cossonerie, Saint Geneviève des Bois. The Russian House is a home where 250 retired Russian refugees can be accommodated. Aleksandr Feodorovich Kerensky publishes his book, *The Catastrophe*, his own story about the Russian Revolution.

· From Alexandra Rakhmanova's diary, **August 22, 1927**: A letter from my mother, "Father is arrested and thrown into a dungeon. I don't know why. He hopes it's a misunderstanding." August 24: Out of the gatherings of old and young Russian writers in the salon is the writer Dmitri Merezhkovsky and his wife Zinaida Hippius; 'The Green Lamp' comes into being, a literary circle with a respectable number of members.

· **Nice, France, September 14**: After finishing her book *My Life*, the dancer Isadora Duncan dies in a car, just like her children Deirdre and Patrick. Her long scarf gets stuck in the spokes of her car, and literally strangles her. Isadora Duncan caused a stir by appearing on stage barefooted and only dressed in a tunic. In 1922 Isadora married the Russian poet Serge Esenin. They met in February 1921 when Isadora danced with the Bolshoy Theatre in Moscow. From 1921 to 1924 she had a school of dance in Moscow. December 28: The writer and poet Serge Alexandrovich Esenin (1895-1925), who was married to Isadora Duncan, is in Russia and criticized for his shocking statements, commits suicide in Hotel Angleterre in Petrograd (St. Petersburg).

· **Paris, December 3**: The Russian cabaret Shéhérazade, 3 Rue de Liège, opens its doors. (The establishment became world famous by Erich Maria Remarque's novel *Arch of Triumph*, and the film of the same name in 1948 with Charles Boyer and Ingrid Bergman in the leading parts.)

· **January 31, 1928**: Stalin has ordered Leo Trotsky to leave Alma Ata. Trotsky is banished to the isle of Prinkipo in Turkey. From the beginning of May to August 8 Anastasia Nikolaevna Romanoff lives in the house of her cousin, Grand Duchess Xenia Grigorievna.

· **May 27, 1928**: Xenia states in *World* magazine, "I am convinced that she is the daughter of Nicholas II. I have often played with Anastasia; she has my age. Mrs. Chaikovsky has surprised me completely by arousing the memories of what we did and said in our childhood. I'm absolutely sure of her identity and I'm prepared to put my whole capital at stake to prove that she is Anastasia." It is of no avail. Forty-four members of the House of Romanoff are still alive. A family council is held, in which it's proposed to sign a statement against Anastasia; thirty-two members of the family refuse to sign the statement, the twelve who sign it are coincidentally the direct heirs when it can be proven that none of the children of the tsar is still alive: Xenia Alexandrovna and her husband Alexander, Olga Alexandrovna and her second husband Nicholas Kulikovsky (1881-1958), the six sons of Alexander and Xenia, their daughter Irina and Irina's husband Felix Yussupov. Several million English pounds are at stake.

Also important was the role of the Russian-Orthodox Church outside of Russia, which had canonized the entire Imperial family, and was in a tight corner when it became clear that Anastasia was still alive and anything but a saint. Anastasia knew who she was, and that was good enough for her. That, and her confabulations, filling the gap of missing information in the own memory with common known facts or the memories of others, have cooked her goose during the many lawsuits about her identity, because during the years the "facts" changed, and if she "lied" about one thing, she most likely didn't tell the truth about other things.

· **October 14**: Grand Duke Nicholas Nikolaevich Romanoff, who lived in Antibes until July 1923, after which he moved to the Chateau de Choigny in Santeny, near Paris, returns to the Villa Thénard; he is seriously ill, and he wants to be near his brother Peter.

· **Paris, October 24**: Prince Felix Yussupov and his wife Irina found their fashion house Irfé (Irina-Felix), on the second floor. (Are they expecting some money, perhaps?) Almost their entire staff consists of Russian refugees. Successively they open branches in Touquet, London and Berlin. The Yussupovs live in the Rue Pierre Guérin. (*Trivia: That house was demolished. Only a green garden door with a door bell and a sign `Chien mechant' is left of the old building.*) October 25: Maria Solovyov, a daughter of Rasputin, institutes legal proceedings against Prince Felix Yussupov and Grand Duke Dmitri Pavlovich Romanoff. She demands a compensation of twenty-five million francs because the gentlemen have murdered her father. The French court however considers itself not cognizant to deal with this case. London, October 26: Dima Ignatieff returns to England and takes his mother and his brothers Lionel and George with him to Canada. His father Paul stays in Paris.

· **New York, October 27**: Igor Sikorsky becomes an American citizen. His first real American success is the S-38 (Amphibian). The S-38 is so successful that Sikorsky has to move to Connecticut, where his company is taken over by the United Aircraft Company, in which Sikorsky becomes one of the managers. Successively he works on the development of long-range flying boats.

· **Copenhagen, November**: Dowager Empress Maria Feodorovna Romanoff (1847-1928) dies at the age of seventy-two. In 1919, she escaped from Russia with the British warship Marlborough, together with her daughters Xenia and Olga and their families. She returned to Denmark (she was born Princess Dagmar of Denmark) and since then lived in a wing of the palace of her cousin, the Danish King Christian X. King George V of England granted her a pension of 10,000 pounds per year. Paris, November 18: Drama critic Lev (Dominique) Aronson opens a Russian restaurant at the address 19 Rue Bréa. The Russian writers who frequent the restaurant Dominique call themselves 'the Dominicans.'

· **November 19**: Count Alexander Buxhoeveden is a developer in Paris, and because his business is doing well, he and his family move to Nice.

· **January 5, 1929**: Grand Duke Nicholas Nikolaevich Romanoff dies. January 7: Vera Bunin writes in her diary, "The funeral ceremony lasted almost an hour. Ivan (Bunin) was very touched, especially when the Cossacks in uniform arrived to form the guard of honor. He did not hold back his tears. We felt that we were committing Old Russia to the ground. Surely we realize that all this will pass, but our wounds are hardly healed, and Nicholas Nikolaevich' death teared them open again, and that hurts, that really hurts."

· **Paris, February 10**: The theater, Intime Russe, opens with the play *Wolves and Sheep* by Alexander Nikolaevich Ostrovsky (1823-1886). The small theatre is headed by D. Kirova, an artist of the former Small Theatre of St. Petersburg. March 16: Tatiana Souchotin Tolstoy, the eldest daughter of Lev Tolstoy, opens a Russian art academy in the Rue Jules Chaplain. However, due to a lack of pupils, the school has to close down. *(Trivia: Nowadays the ballet school of the Russian, Irina Gryebina, is located there.)* May 22: Igor Sikorsky turns back to his first love: the development of the helicopter. June 5: The composer Serge Sergeevich Prokofyev (1891-1953) moves to Haüy, Paris, where he will live until 1932. Serge is a child prodigy and had already played the piano when he was only three years old. He was a pupil of Glière, Liadov, and Rimsky-Korsakov, worked with Diaghilev in London and Paris since 1914, and since 1917, has given numerous concerts all over Europe, America and Japan. June 18: Marina Tsvetaeva publishes her essay "Natalia Goncharova" in the paper *Liberté de la Russie*. Tsvetaeva met the painters Larionov and Goncharova in Café de Flore, Paris, where she offered to write a story about them. October 27: Grand Duke Michael Mikhaïlovich Romanoff (1861-1929), brother of Sandro, dies in London, where he lived during the summers. He was a colonel of the Caucasian tirailleurs. Living for a long time in Cannes, Michael Mikhaïlvich was married to Countess Sophie de Torby, a granddaughter of Pushkin. November 2: Tatiana Nikolaevna Masalitinov and her husband Vladimir emigrate from Bulgaria to France. Shortly afterwards the rest of her family joins her in Besanton, where Vladimir works at a metallurgical factory. Tatiana Nikolaevna's father dies.

· **January 1930**: General Kutiepov, who since April 1928, after the death of General Vrangel, was the president of the ROVS (Union of Russian Veterans in France), lives in Rousselet, Paris. After Kutiepov left his house on January 26, 1930, nobody had seen or heard anything of him. His story, and the one of his successor General De Miller, who was struck by the same unenviable lot, is told in the book *Le général meurt à minuit*, by Marina Grey, the daughter of General Denikin.

· **January 9**: In London Oleg Olegovich Kerensky, the son of Oleg Alexandrovich and Nathalie, is born. Grandfather Alexander Kerensky comes to visit the newborn.

· **Paris, April 22**: Grand Duke Kiril Vladimirovich Romanoff takes the salute of 2,000 former officers of the Imperial Army. The officers shout out Cossack war cries and, "The day of victory is near!"

· **January 17, 1931**: Grand Duke Peter Nikolaevich Romanoff (1864-1931), a brother of Grand Duke Nicholas Nikolaevich and uncle of Tsar Nicholas, dies in Cap d'Antibes, France. Peter Nikolaevich was married to Princess Militsa of Montenegro. He was a Lieutenant-General in the Cavalry and aide-de-camp to Nicholas II.

· **July 30**: The British playwright George Bernard Shaw, 74, is an admirer of the Soviet system, like so many 'progressive' Western writers. When he visits Moscow, he says, "Tomorrow I leave the land of hope, to return to the Western lands of despair." Shaw talked for more than two hours with Stalin. The Soviet Union is also glorified by the famous Dutch writer Henriëtte Roland Holst-Van der Schalk, after whom in Holland streets are named. In her book *Foundations and Problems of the New Culture in Soviet-Russia* (1932), she writes, "One wants to create a new, entirely on one principle imbued culture. Such attempts can only succeed in a stage of very strong rationalized thinking. Also it can only be exercised in a society in which the main means of culture (school, press, publishers, bookstores, theatre, film, radio) are controlled by a central authority. This systematically ruled society includes also that the new form of living is much less than before to be found in friendly cooperation, but in a system, cut and dried by the leaders, which is imposed on the subordinates. In this respect the coming culture in Russia is aristocratical. When the children of the farmers now say, 'There is no God,' then, in a way, they speak the truth. The old Russian God, who was attached to a perished world, a world of random and cruelty, of haughtiness and arrogance, of humility and servility, that old God does no more exist. He was knocked to the ground, together with his earthly representative, the tsar. And with him perished a world of half-moldered notions, of rigid morality, which had gotten into a groove."

One is tempted to think that Mrs. Roland Holst is misled, that she does not know what's she's talking about, but that notion is not correct. When she commits her Stalinist propaganda to paper, she is positively well informed about the abuses, but with her it's the same as with a lot of other European and American armchair revolutionaries: facts are neglected for the sake of ideals. She writes, "The health of the working youth is also undermined by night shifts, which is reinstated for large groups of young workers. In the textiles area of Ivanovo Vosnosensk (in February 1930) out of 1,664 youthful workers 972 worked at night. In lots of plants they have to do night shifts, inter alia in the glass industry, food industry and shoe-factories. There's also child labour in branches of industry which are injurious to health. The 'Youth Pravda' of February 10, 1930, from which comes this data, stated in fact that the health of the children is very bad. In Siberia 4,000 out of less than 6,000 youthful workers had to be treated medically. Most likely the present conditions are still not much improved."

· **Nice, Southern France, June 2**: Count Anatol (Alec) Buxhoeveden (1905-1970s), the eldest son of Count Alexander Buxhoeveden, marries Vera Illarionov, daughter of Count Nicholas Illarionov and Countess Natalia Peresviat-Soltan. June 18: Nobody is willing to donate any more money to the Russian Red Cross, and that's why Paul Ignatieff joins his wife and children in Toronto. However, Paul and Natasha have virtually grown apart.

· **February 26, 1933**: Grand Duke Alexander (Sandro) Mikha-ïlovich Romanoff (1866-1933), an old friend of Tsar Nicholas, dies in his villa Sainte-Thérèse in Roquebrune, France.

· **March 21**: Lincoln Kirstein brings the famous Russian choreographer George Balanchine from Paris to New York. A couple of months later Balanchine, who since 1928 worked with Igor Strawinsky, founds the New York City Ballet.

· **June 3**: When Prince Alexis Alexeevich Obolensky reaches New York, his mother, Princess Lyubova Obolensky, née Troubetzkoy (1909-1980), who has a real head for business, opens the first of her successful American enterprises, which boom on Park Avenue. As 'Princess Obolensky Incorporated,' she retails quilts, bed covers and pillows. Later she expands and exhibits her wares in all the social resorts. Prince Alexis himself starts out as a perfume salesman.

· **August**: The archives of the prohibited Scouting Club Ruskii Skautizm were smuggled to Odessa. After the Whites were defeated some loyal scouts hid the archives, but last month they were caught and imprisoned. Nothing was heard of them since. To prevent that the names in the archives can be used to try (former) illegal scouts, the archives are stolen from the secret police and moved to Moscow by some former scouts, who became officers in the Red Army. They hide the archives in the basements of the Ministry of Defense. *(Trivia: That's where they still are today, in remembrance of all the murdered scouts.)*

· **August 11**: Count Alexander Buxhoeveden and Countess Olga Buxhoeveden, née Olensky, are divorced in Sremsky Karlovci, Yugoslavia, by the Synod of the Russian Orthodox Church outside of Russia.

· **September**: Vladimir Smirnoff has financial difficulties and is forced to sell the Smirnoff brand and the secret vodka formula to the Russian refugee Rudolph Kunnett, who lives in the United States.

· **Paris, September 24**: Count Alexander Buxhoeveden marries Rosine-Marie Vidal (1911-present), daughter of engineer Paul Vidal and Germaine-Marie Delvoueuillerie de Costaire. Nice and Southern France, July 1, 1934: Count Theodor Buxhoeveden (1934-1965), Count Alexander's first son out of his marriage to Rosine-Marie Vidal, is born, and Aleksandr Feodorovich Kerensky publishes his book *The Crucifixion of Liberty*.

· **September 12**: After General Yuri Daniloff dies in Paris, his wife Anna leaves for America to see after her grandchildren.

· **Paris, November 21**: At 8 p.m., a 25-year-old Russian poet falls off the platform on the railway, in the subway-station Pasteur. He is run over and transported to the Necker Hospital, where he succumbs to his wounds at 10 p.m. On account of this accident Tsvetaeva writes a letter to her friend Anne Teskov. "On November 21 Nicholas Gronsky has been run over by a subway-train. When we saw each other for the first time, he fell in love with me instantly; it took some time before I fell in love with him. This love lasted a year, but because I found that my freedom was rather limited by it, and because our ways of life rather differed, we grew apart. In the spring of 1931 we said goodbye for good. In three years time I've only seen him one more time, in a subway train. I called him, but he didn't come to me. And then I read in the newspapers what had happened on November 21." Due to the fact that Russia didn't sign the Bern Convention, Strawinsky can't claim royalties and copyrights. Had he been German, French or American, then he would have been a rich man.

· **Leningrad, December 1**: Serge Kirov, the secretary of the Communist Party in Leningrad, is killed in the Smolny Institute by Leonid Nikolaev. This way Nikolaev, an embittered communist, wanted to draw attention to the deterioration and officialism of the party. Moscow/Leningrad, December 6: In connection with the murder of Serge Kirov, many people are executed in Moscow and Leningrad. Start of the Big Terror.

· **Paris, December 13**: Countess Marianna Buxhoeveden (1913-), daughter of Count Alexander, marries the Russian nobleman Vladimir Vassiliev (1907-1987). Nice, Southern France, June 29: Count Alexander Alexandrovich Buxhoeveden, Count Alexander's second son out of his second marriage, is born. March 28: The Buxhoevedens move to Florence, Italy, where Count Alexander Alexandrovich is baptized. Allassio, Italy, July 16: Countess Rosine-Marie Buxhoeveden (1938-2003), Count Alexander's first daughter out of his second marriage, is born. She will be called Rosemarie. Merano, Italy, October 18: Countess Catherine Geneviève Buxhoeveden (1939-), Count Alexander's second daughter out of his second marriage, is born. Nice, Southern France, December: Countess Elisabeth Buxhoeveden, Count Alexander's first daughter out of his first marriage, marries the Russian nobleman Vladimir Panov (1880-1945). The Buxhoevedens emigrate from Italy to the United States. On September 30, their son Count Daniel Paul Buxhoeveden (1947-present) is born in Great Neck, New York. New York, May 11: Count Alexander Buxhoeveden dies. Countess Vera Buxhoeveden, the wife of Count Anatol (Alec), his eldest son, takes charge of young Alexander, her brother-in-law. She and father Anthony von Grabbe are instrumental in getting Alexander into the Holy Trinity Monastery in Jordanville, New York. Countess Vera organizes the annual ball of the Russian Nobility Association in America.

· **New York, September 10**: Countess Rosine-Marie Buxhoeveden, née Vidal, marries the private teacher Hans Kessler (1899-1976). New York, September 17: Count Anatol (Alec) Buxhoeveden, Count Alexander's eldest son, divorces his wife, Countess Vera Buxhoeveden, née Illarionov. New York, April 21, 1959:

Count Anatol (Alec) Buxhoeveden marries Miss Roberta (Bobby) Montague Rose (1907). Miss Rose was born in London, a daughter of the banker Archibald Adolph Rose and Francis Lake Montague. She is the widow of publisher Thomas Leaman (1904-1951), whom she married in Palma de Mallorca, Spain, on January 3, 1933. Noroton, Connecticut, September 29, 1962: Countess Catherine Geneviève Buxhoeveden, Count Alexander's second daughter out of his second marriage, marries the author, composer and parapsychologist Hans Holzer, from Vienna, Austria. Jerusalem: Count Alexander Alexandrovich Buxhoeveden, Count Alexander's second son out of his second marriage who was a lay brother in the Holy Trinity Monastery in Jordanville, New York for seven years, before going in 1961 to Jerusalem with Father Anthony von Grabbe, is forced to return to New York due to an accident. The only things Count Alexander and Countess Maria have of the Buxhoeveden heirlooms are a plate on their wall, one of a set that Catherine the Great gave to an ancestor, and a tiny icon of Alexander Nevsky.

That was hard to do without speaking, but now I must say a few things here. First off, Catherine has a couple of the gold plates with the family crest and they are magnificent. Rosine handed them out to her surviving children, as she was passing on their father's legacy. Secondly Vera and Alec were not very kind people. When Rosine came to the United Sates with four small children and one on the way, she knew no one. She only spoke French and Italian and had very little. The war left the Count in a weakened state and it wasn't soon after he passed from a heart attack, once again leaving Rosine in a crisis but now in a foreign land with five children. From the Count's first marriage, his son Alec and his cold wife Vera were already settled in Great Neck, Long Island. When it came time to call upon them for help, they turned their backs on Rosine and the children. Rosine needed to leave right away.

During the period between May and October of 1948 the family moved from place to place. Finally, she had to separate the children. Two girls, Catherine and Rosemarie, were placed in one foster home and the boys in another, while she took a room with the new baby. That was my Uncle Danny. Rosine was able to get assistance through an Italian acquaintance from Social Services who found an old house in Lynbrook, Long Island. Rosine said yes and the family reunited in October that same year. Rosine recounts her life growing up in a later chapter. The truth is told at last and sets free many disturbed souls. What is the Russian spirit? Perhaps a photo in front of the Novodichi Convent in Moscow. Perhaps a visit to the church of a great-grandfather in the Ukrain. For this family member living today, it is the icon of the Mother of God of Kazan, combined with the sound of Orthodox hymns. Keep searching and you will find it. Perhaps the Russian spirit is a web, in which one can be caught. One thing's for sure: the Russian spirit is a cultural thing, and it cannot be inherited by blood alone. A Russian who is born in an African jungle and raised like any other African, will never know what the Russian spirit is unless he will search for it and experience it.

Michael Ignatieff's grandfather was the last Minister of Education under the Tsar. Michael was born in Canada. Count Pavel, his grandfather, died there. Michael grew up as a Canadian kid, a non-believer. Recently he went to the Ukrain, to visit the Orthodox church his great-grandfather built. At the grave of his great-grandfather, in church (during the famine the grave was used as a butcher's block), Michael said, 'Your home is where your graves are.' A few hours later he was completely overwhelmed by the beautiful Orthodox singing in the church, and that was the first time in all his life he experienced the Russian spirit. He was caught in the web, in the endless catacombs of what we call the 'Russian spirit.' Mind you, I love to be there, but you have to realize you can never leave. Most important: entering the Russian spirit is a quest for the inner man or woman. You may not like what you will find there, but once confronted with it, you have to deal with it. The Russian spirit knows high mountains and deep valleys, higher and deeper than any European or American spirit. Sure, melancholy is a part of the Russian spirit, but so is joy and laughter; they keep each other in balance, like yin and yang. A Russian is inclined to let himself be dragged down by his emotions. If those emotions are pure and straight from the heart then so what of it? In our society one can only hear too often, "control yourself, don't get carried away." Why not? Because this way the outer world will see the inner man? What's wrong with that? There is a lot going on here when it comes to my family. Hans and Catherine come from very different times, as they are twenty years apart. However, historically, Catherine bears all the weight here and so, it is here where I continue on the Royal Russian legacy.

Little Russia in New York: The Russian aristocracy is only a very small part of the total Russian population of New York. The majority of the Russian emigrants and their descendants go out every morning with their lunch boxes, to the office or the plant. Of course their history is no less sad than the one of the aristocracy. This is as honest as it can get about families surviving wars and poverty only to continue on their heritage and lineage. The first Russian emigrants wave of this century was in the early 1920s. After the October Revolution of 1917 more than a million people escaped from Russia. Many of them did not go to America directly, but stayed some years in Europe first, particularly in France. This first wave brought the Russian culture to New York. Some remains of this community can still be found between East 60th and East 96th Street, but probably not for long. As with anything, change is inevitable — and construction sites are popping up all over Manhattan.

The second Russian emigrants wave arrived in the United States towards the end of the 1940s, mainly from Germany, where many of them had been in Displaced Persons camps. Especially for elderly people it was very hard to start their lives in a new country, with a completely different language. My grandmother, Rosine, being one of them with four small children and a fifth on the way. *Can you even begin to surmise what hell she and countless others like her were going through? And, they didn't have washer machines or dishwashers either, so I think as a society we need to take a step back and look at that for a moment. Look at that fact and reflect on the errors of our ways and see how perhaps we could be better people. There is always something someone could do better if they have a second chance or start anew the next day.* Most of them worked as maids, cleaning women, and mill hands; in other words: where there was no need to speak good English. The younger generation went to school and later they worked in offices or, if their parents could afford it, continued studying in universities and pursuing a higher education. The computer field is very popular among this generation.

Some Russians were welcomed with open arms by the American government because of certain knowledge they had of communist society, and others worked for the anti-communist radio station "The Voice of America," which broadcasted in Eastern Europe, but many had to take odd jobs. The second Russian emigrants wave mainly settled down in and around Glen Cove, Long Island, which since has developed as a real Russian enclave. Besides the Cathedral of the Ascension, on Old Tappan Road there are some smaller Russian-Orthodox churches, which have been built by the emigrants themselves. On the streets almost everyone speaks Russian, and everywhere around you, you can see Russian stores, people reading Russian newspapers, et cetera. Nearby, in Roslyn, is a Russian cemetery.

Chapter Twenty:

THE WOMAN BEHIND THE COUNT

I would now like to introduce you to the woman who bore my mother and help continue a Royal Legacy. Hold on because this is an emotional ride and hauntingly sad indeed. I must have received dozens of phone calls from Rosine when she heard I was including this part into the memoir. The poor dear has relived all of what you are about to read but, it is crucial in the understanding of fated paths and the harshness and beauty of the spiritual life Hans talks about.

"He's not a handsome man, but has a handsome personality. A strong person who had a presence about him. He was easy to talk with and was very Russian. He had a way with the ladies as he always was polite in kissing their hands and pulling out their chairs," recounts Rosine at the young age of ninety-seven.

And so began her life path as she reflected back to a time before meeting Alexander. "When the events of life pass again before my eyes, it resembles a puppet show, the funniest incidents or the most dramatic, vanish with time. I would like to retrace the most important events because time passes quickly, life escapes us, and one would love to be able to catch the flight of departed stolen youth. One of the profound images of childhood was when I was a little more than two years old and my parents separated. My father took my sister and myself to his parents, to a well known bourgeois apartment. The large apartment was well furnished, but somber and sad with aged, disagreeable grandparents. I remember that as a flashback like an old film where my father's departure and us staying there had my sister crying. I do not think that I cried. In any case, I learned very quickly to hold back my tears and not show my distress. I can scarcely remember the days that followed, being very young.

"But the War of 1914 arrived and shortly after my father left for the front, where he lost his life. After that we were sent to a convent; not having bad memories because I was very young, around four and a half. The nuns were very, very good to me. I didn't study… I would run in the garden that surrounded the convent and would play with the rosaries. These were my toys given to me by the sisters. I still see them; blue, red, white and green. It wasn't necessary to make noise in order to disturb classes. Because of the bombardments of Paris, our grandparents took us for long months near the sea. We stayed there until the armistice.

"Our childhood was not bad, materially. We were all fed, lodged and dressed. The doctor was called when we were ill. I believe our grandparents were all they could be. Only we suffered from spiritual suffocation, the lack of gaiety, of youth, of feeling undesirable, and of suffering unending and unreasonable criticism. I certainly was their target as I resembled my mother… our mother who they never accepted. During the years spent at the convent, which we had preferred to those at home, we were the happiest being in the company of girls all ages. The Sisters were gentle with us. My first sister was Sister Genevieve. She was still very young, happy, and loving. She occupied herself with the young and loved me very much. The assistant director, Sister Marie Therese, was full of goodness and indulgence. The Mother Superior was a great lady of distinction. Yes, we regretted it when we had to leave the convent before finishing our studies. Why? We knew that the war and the Russian Revolution had left us in ruins! After that, grandfather put himself in charge of our education. He was very erudite and we were very good students, always certainly in history, geography, and literature. Paulette my sister, was better in calculus and design than I. Therefore, the long and monotonous years passed between caring for the house. We no longer had a housekeeper (only a chairwoman). Our paternal grandparents played an important role in our lives as our mother was an orphan herself. They were very different in nature, tastes, and education."

On her Grandfather

"Bourgeois, informed and well educated, which did not prevent him from being disagreeable at will. My grandmother, also orphaned at an early age, had been raised liberal enough for the time by friends of her mother. We never knew how our grandparents met each other, but they remained married for fifty years. As a child, I remember them aged, as all adults to me looked that way. My grandfather occupied himself with books and clocks, leaving those in each room in the large apartment. He would go to the Observatory of Paris to set the time. Especially this one beautiful gold watch because in France, we had two times: the exact and the inexact. When we traveled in a small town or village for vacations, he would ask someone, 'Oh, do you have the exact time?' Briefly, he would return home to set the clocks and watches to the proper time. What a racket that made in the night. Even grandmother was not able to stop him. I think for that reason my sister and I have an aversion to clocks and watches! There is a poem Paulette loved to read written by Baudelaire called "L'Horlodge," which began: 'Watch, sinister, frightening, immovable God, then the finger menaces and tell us, you remember. Three thousand six hundred times an hour, the second ticks. You remember, rapid rapid with his voice of an insect. Now says, I am from another time. And I have exhausted your life with my impure blast. Presently will sound the time of the divine chance, where the august virtue, your still virgin spouse. Or the same repentant (oh the last auberge). Or all will tell you, die, old shameful one, it is too late.'

"As a youth, grandfather wanted to be a painter, but to his horror became a geometric engineer. His sketching ability was always good and I remember his talent very well. His love of history equaled his love of clocks. Napoleon was one of his heroes. He knew the Napolenic epoch by heart as well as the history of France and Europe. Another weakness is old Paris. He loved to talk with us about the old streets called the mazars. He'd recount the deeds that took place in those streets. The old hotels, those of Joseph Balsamo (Gagliostro), Cardinal of Rohan, the fountain of Olovier of Clisson and others.

On her Grandmother

Tiny, plumpish, fresh rosy skin, greying hair and large black eyes. She was hard, but beautiful just the same. When her eyes gazed upon us in anger, my sister and I would escape underground. Full of quality, she was devoted and very commanding. Raised freely, she had been independent before her marriage. If there had been women's liberation at this time, she would certainly have volunteered in criticizing men... All but her son-in-law who she adored. Grandmother Josephine was her name and neither took part in grandfather's taste for art, books or museums. She was practical and enjoyed business and properties. Eating and drinking well, she was also a gourmet cook as most of the French are. When fruits were in season, she would go with the housemaid Leonie to the Halles Market early in the morning. They would return with baskets full of fragrant fruits. During these days, all households made their own jams.

Vacations

Sometimes we'd go to the sea, one place was called Sable of Olone. I remember amusing episodes where grandmother was filling up trunks and valises as if we were moving. Grandfather would complain that he'd have to pay for more excessive baggage. The day of departure we squeezed into a taxi as each of us were assigned to carry a specific item. Grandmother was in charge of toiletries. I was in charge of umbrellas, which were wrapped in an elegant fourreau de cuir. This way it prevented all the umbrellas from mixing up with parasols and canes. It was cumbersome to drag. My sister had the covers for the trip. Grandfather had a servant carry the large valises. Fortunately our place was reserved and we looked forward to the beach and swimming. We rented a small donkey cart from the neighboring countryside. In the beautiful Vendenne countryside after lunch we gathered mulberries. Our mouths went black after eating them, but they were delicious. When we departed for the capital, we had to lug everything again. Grandmother made syrup and put them in well-sealed bottles placed in a basket. Sitting in a beautiful first class compartment decorated in red velour, we took off on the train. The syrup placed over grandfather fell and poured all over him. We were not capable of moving because the crazy laughter overtook all three of us. Another time, traveling East, we took a train between Nancy and Met. After lugging once again all the valises, a conductor came out and said we had gotten on the wrong train. We would have to leave. Grandfather was angry.

These grandparents who seemed so good-natured nevertheless sometimes were hard on us and made us suffer. They would say it was in order to teach us about life. They were unaware of the sensitivity of children and of the marks they could leave. The last fond childhood memory I wish to share is that I had a favorite doll I named Gaby. It was a plastic 'swimmer' and I swam with her in the ocean. One day grandfather crushed it, throwing it at the window. Something or someone irritated him and we never knew why. One night during the war, we were going to the cellar. I realized Gaby wasn't with me. I had to run about the darkened apartment bumping into things while the sirens were shrieking outside. My grandparents were furiously calling me. I could not leave that doll. Mortified in the stairway I was indifferent to their reproaches, hugging Gaby in my arms.

Leaving the Convent

Years passed slowly between the convent and the last of our vacations. Everything became fewer: the vacations, the visitors, and the embroidery, so we turned more to reading. My mother since had remarried after my father went MIA. We never did know how he died as they never found him. The only bright spot at that time was the marriage of my cousin Odette, where we spent a summer in Belgium. Odette's new family brought about fun and we admired the beaches of Ostente, Blankenberg. In the month of August, its beauty was surrounded by cold winds nonetheless. Bruges was another beautiful memory. Bruges, the death as one called the silent canals. The museums and churches were typically Flemish. Flemish art work and the superb Van Dycks were all around. The memlings made me ecstatic. All of a sudden where there was silence, many church clocks began to chime bringing back haunting memories.

Odette was the only daughter and spoiled by her parents. She was intelligent, an egoist with large brown eyes and auburn hair. Her face was not bad, but too fat and not very gracious or attractive. When she married Jacques in 1924, it was a marriage of arrangement by the families. Jacques' father was an old colonel of The Republican Guard. His wife was of petty nobility, but very talented in music and art. After the honeymoon, the house they rented to live in remained vacant. Instead Odette and Jacques moved into her parents house. After six months, Jacques left. Before this marriage, Jacques had an affair with a married woman and perhaps accepted this arrangement with Odette to escape. Some years later we learned that Jacques remarried and left for the colonies to seek his fortune. And so I began to keep a journal to keep sane. August 10, 1928: Excursion to Rochefort, visiting the house of 'Pierre Loti.' Simple outside and grand on the inside with treasures he had purchased from distant countries.

August 18: Walking in Trembelade, Oyster County, where we ate many. Grandmother adores oysters and was in very good humor. We even made her get a permanent at a local hairdresser's. August 20: Today we did nothing. Staying in the garden. The house had been transformed in 1925, a second floor had been added. August 25: Evening at the casino. Theater, dancing and a game room where we saw Sacha Guitry and Yvonne Printemps who were very well known actors and writers. September 2: Grandmother, in good humor, became unpleasant as grandfather grumbled throughout the summer. September 10: The last family guests of Sevarac left. Arriving was a doctor who Grandfather could not stand. This doctor was a bachelor and flirted with all the women. I didn't like him much, but what could I do? He was a friend of the family of the Duviver's. September 15: After the departure of my uncle, the grandparents became impossible with all of us. My sister helped my grandmother every morning, to dress her and do her hair. Paulette would then get the brunt of her moods. Paulette loses sleep and her appetite. September 22: We have had enough of this life. We speak seriously with our aunt. What can we do to free ourselves from their guardianship? She promised to help. September 23: Nothing special today. My sister is seventeen and I am twelve and I can't help thinking, is this it? September 24: Such conspiracy with my parents and the anger my grandparents harbored towards our mother. It took Paulette's first communion to bring my mother together with them again. September 25: I dare not write anything as the doctor is leaving on the morning train and us later in the evening. What is going to happen? September 28: Finally a bit of calm. After the train's departure for Paris, my aunt discharged the chauffeur, saying that we would return on foot. Instead we took a small train, which followed the coast and went as far as possible. It was a beautiful walk, but we were so nervous that we barely looked at the countryside. Had lunch by the sea, then ran onto the beach trying to laugh and have fun. When evening fell, we returned to Royan and stayed at a hotel on the promenade. Only our aunt and the cook, who secretly was with the doctor, had our trust. It was arranged that she would put a lit lamp in the front window facing the Boulevard, showing us if the grandparents were gone. If not, a handkerchief was tied across the window. After dinner, we couldn't wait a moment longer and took a walk near the villa. The lamp was on, but to be on the safe side we returned to the hotel. The next morning we were told that the grandparents were furious. We left.

October 1: It is strange to find ourselves without the grandparents watching over us. October 2: We close up the villa. Tomorrow we're leaving in a Cadillac with the chauffeur, our aunt and her small dogs. October 3: We arrived in the evening just outside of Paris. Our uncle was happy to see us. He was a bit worried about the grandparents and what they were going to do? End of October: The letters that were sent from my aunt and sister remained without answer. The grandparents were really angry. Our uncle went to see them and told us that they were in need of nothing and if necessary the concierge would contact them. January of 1929: I no longer write in my journal. We are too occupied taking business courses. April: Winter passed quickly. We were making some friends and remaining close with our cousins. One cousin had raised his family in the modern way at the time. This way was to teach the children to take value in their beauty and only to marry wealthy. One month later, grandmother passes. When we were contacted in the middle of the night, upon arriving at their hotel, it was too late. My aunt didn't want to deal with her father, my grandfather, so Paulette thus decided to return to live with him. Obviously, I followed her, against my wishes but on the condition I finish my studies and find a [job]. My uncle and aunt accepted that plan. I felt let down a bit by them, but what could we do. Grandfather was left with this apartment and didn't want to leave. With his income, he could have found someone better suited for his care. The death of grandmother reunited grandfather with his brother Louis with whom he'd been angry with since the death of their father. It was over the inheritance. Until now, my uncle Louis and his wife didn't even know we had existed. Funny family. Whenever we stayed out at night with the new cousins, we tried to laugh quietly as not to attract attention. True to my promise in finding [work], I had an offer to be a salesperson with one of Paulette's friend's mother. She had a fashion boutique for children in Ternes and nice clientele. I spent a year there and it helped vanquish any intimidation I had felt growing up.

In the summer of 1930, the boutique closed. We departed to Pouligen. It was there where I would have my first kiss with a boy named Jacques. After the return to Paris, Jacques sent correspondence, saying he was in Cologne to perfect his German. We had decided to wait to marry, having dreams of going to the colonies and Tahiti. He always wanted me to introduce him to grandfather, but I didn't and, as a result, when grandfather learned of [our relationship], he made us separate. Upon finding another [job] and moving on with my life, I became a model for clothes for girls and the days were long. Paulette had a boyfriend, but he didn't finish his studies, so it was not allowed to continue. As I was being pricked by pins, I didn't move and did well for the designers. April of 1931: This thought of Pascal falls under my eyes corresponding to the state of my soul. Being bored, nothing's more intolerable than to be in full repose without passion. Without things to do, without diversions or applications. Feeling your nothingness, inadequacies, dependency... it leaves the soul with grief, sadness and despair. Our nature is in movement and complete rest is death. It is because of this that I hate Sundays and holidays. During the week at least I am occupied, but Sundays are endless. Life went on with grandfather.

A Sad Love Story

I met George. He had been a pilot during the war and told me of his regret of no longer flying. We tread on dead leaves, were very romantic, and exchanged ideas. George had this [vision] of purchasing a pleasure aircraft. I told him these planes are not safe. I saw his death as a result. He gave me a look. September 22: I was slipped a note that George wrote, but it was not written that way. I recognized his signature. He wishes to see me and misses me. Not knowing my exact address what was his plan? October: This morning in the metro, dark eyes are looking at me. Oh no, my God it's him! He had to get up early because he lived so far away from me. He approached me trying to speak. It was impossible with the commotion all around. We got off at the next station and took a taxi. He still declared his love for me. To my objections, he swears he has never lied to me despite what I had heard. We got out of the taxi, standing there. Deciding nothing, I went my way and he, his. A couple of weeks later he wrote my sister, begging to meet. We did and Paulette liked him. He wrote of the plans of our future that he could make for me. Grandfather must not know. We continued on with our relationship. We were twenty years apart; I was twenty and he, forty, but despite the age difference, loved one another. His was ready for the engagement, but pressed on my family's side because of grandfather. He wanted me to quit my modeling job, but I said only when I am engaged. It didn't work out due to distance and so many circumstances.

The winter of 1932 would be the longest year for me trying to forget George. When spring arrived, he tried to contact me at my aunt's. Having sons from a previous marriage, he wanted to make this work for us. I found him still very engaging — his kisses were warm and tender, now I have decided to marry him. But he didn't seem right. I later found out why after one of our visits. I received a long letter asking me to forgive him and begging me to become his mistress while we wait. 'Wait for what?' I asked. One of his sons was in college and so he was pulled in many directions. It would be weeks until we met again. I missed him. We were both extremely sad as we met. Life always appeared complicated to me. We separated that time and I feared it would be the last I'd ever see of him. He called my aunt's house later on telling me he bought his plane, even though I begged him not to. I had a premonition of his death, he laughed it off. Months later, I opened up a newspaper and saw his picture. The headline read, "An Industrialist, Monsieur George killed himself in his airplane." This was due to fog and he collided with another aircraft containing two passengers. "No survivors."

The Meeting

May 6, 1933: Today I turn twenty-two. I was at the hairdressers when a great and imposing gentleman called for me. My sister arranged a meeting by telephone. As we didn't know one another, this was very funny to me. I went directly to him as if it were natural. He took me to lunch where we made ourselves known to each other. Paulette joined us for desserts. From the start we were very much at ease with him and he with us. He took us to the movies and returned us in a taxi at seven o'clock curfew. May 7: Sunday, happily grandfather has left. We can now see Count Alexander. This time the three of us are going dancing at The Pavilion of Armenonville. While dancing, the count recounts bits of his life. He speaks of the separation with his wife that led to his divorce. We returned at seven o'clock. I saw him the next day after work for an aperitif. He didn't smoke or drink much, so we had orange juice. He loved to tell me he was glad I didn't smoke because his daughters had a bad habit of that. All three of them took after their mother. Then, he had to leave by train, saying he'd write and call when he returned. Mid-May: Sacha, who was the diminutive word for Alexander, wrote me. The letters were sent to another place and each time they were brought to me with roses from Nice. After the flowers came sweetened fruits of Vogade. I offered them at my job, as the box was enormous. He returned to Paris, [staying at the] same hotel called Hotel of Paris. I saw him that Saturday for lunch and Paulette joined us later on. After, in the sitting room of his suite, he asked me to marry him. He wanted to give me a diamond. Not enormous, but beautiful. I cannot accept yet and I asked for time to think. This Sunday, what to do? He is much older than I, but very lively, dynamic, full of health and enthusiasm. He was young at heart and quite opposite of poor George. George was so loving, but so full of doubts and fears. Nothing like that with Sacha, he didn't have a doubt and enough love for two. Paulette wanted me to say yes. I am tempted enough that I make a decision. I am going to take a week's vacation and I will get to know him better.

The Courtship

When he came, I was free to see him from morning to evening for a whole week. Grandfather thought I was working, so it was well planned out. We met each morning in cafes on the boulevards. I am trying to understand his character. Will I be happy with him? Happiness is a lure for me. I already know that he is impulsive, commanding, jealous, but I also know he is generous, gallant, and respectful of women. We share the same idealism of enthusiasm and patriotism. He served his country, suffered, and lost — as all White Russians did. Physically he is very large, strong, and coura- geous. When I am with him, he dominates me and does everything to please me. But his personality tends to make mine disappear as I am already timid by nature. Sometimes that scares me. Some mornings after breakfast, we would go to The Bois de Boulogne walking or taking a boat out on the lake. Then we'd go to antique shops. Sacha loves old furniture and art and so do I. We have the same taste of eighteenth century French. Today we found a marvel- ous bed corbeille 'Marie Antoinette' made out of little points of silk with delicate colors. Later this bed was sold at an auction in New York. Sacha couldn't resist buying this bed for our future bedroom. Afternoons, when it was too hot to run around, we would go to the cinema or to a tea house. He tells me of his life in Russia, his family, ideas, and then the war as he voluntarily entered as a Cos- sack. He was decorated with the Cross of St. George for his valor. Finally, the revolution came and he was arrested several times by the Bolsheviks.

"Sacha," I tell him, "your life is as passionate and interesting as an adventure novel."

"Yes," he replied. "One day we will write it together."

And then he asked me of my parents. Alas, I remember so little as I was only three years old when the war broke out. Father was killed in Argonne during the start of the war. He was an officer and, with three men, charged a reconnaissance mission in enemy lines. Not one of the four returned. Sacha had served in the same war under another flag for the same cause. "And your mother?" he asked. I dreaded this question the most. I told him that I vaguely remember her even though I had seen her several years ago. "My parents," I told him, "separated when I was two." The divorce procedure was never finalized because of the war and his death. Our grandparents adopted and raised us. We knew our mother was trying to see us, but the grandparents refused any visitation from her. Finally she obtained the right to visit and would come and see us at the private boarding school. It was a bad time and I didn't like speaking about it, but Sacha insisted so I continued.

"I remember my mother was tall, beautiful and elegant; brunette with large green eyes, which my sister inherited. I would have liked to been able to love her and to have a mother like other children. We missed [out on] so much affection and were isolated from other family members as a result." I stopped, but Sacha insisted I still go on. "Each Sunday afternoon our mother came to visit. But before that time, grandfather came and made us go into small room [and tried] to brainwash us. I scarcely understood being seven years old. When our mother arrived, no doubt because of the presence of her ex-father in-law, we would go into the parlor. Momma embraced us showering us with affection. Nevertheless we had a sort of a fear from allowing that to feel natural. She gave us candies and cakes that grandfather would take from us. After her departure he'd interrogate us. The result being that each Sunday my sister and I felt sick and nervous. In 1918, because of the bombardment of Paris by the Germans, we left for long months to the sea and never saw mother again." I explained to the count that it wasn't until 1919, that we received a letter of her remarriage to Colonel Chavrondier. He came back from the same war that took our father's life.

July came and Sacha had to leave. I spent an enjoyable week, the first in my life. I accepted the marriage proposal and wore his engagement ring.

Combining a Family

Mid-August: Sacha arrived with his two daughters, having three in a Fiat! Grandfather had just left. We schemed openly over tea and pastries. This evening we would have to advise grandfather. If he made any objections, Sacha declared that he would leave with Paulette and me. We return to the apartment precisely at seven o'clock. Sacha and another stay in the car out front of our property. Grandfather returned late and we impatiently were waiting for him. As soon as he returned, he had no time to take off his shoes when we began our attack. Paulette said, "We want to talk with you." He says, "About what," a bit annoyed. I think he thought we were going to ask questions about his private life as he always went out and came back [without telling us] much of anything. Paulette began the story of Sacha. The questions mounted; what was his age, nationality, religion, divorce? On it went. Meanwhile, I am at the parlor door looking down the hall at my friend showing her so far so good. She then goes down to tell Sacha who's still in the car. Finally, grandfather agrees to meet with him. Paulette won round one because she said Sacha was a Russian in the war losing his fortune to the Bolsheviks. Paulette says to grandfather, "You have something in common. You have lost your fortune, more than hatred of the communists." After Sacha met grandfather, they began to speak of the Russian Revolution and my fiance took all of us out to dinner where his daughters waited impatiently. The result was the dinner was perfect as grandfather even drank champagne to finish the evening. The marriage had been set for September 24. I gave my resignation at work as now I had too much to do. The honeymoon would be in Italy. Happily grandfather disappears more and more as the wedding approaches. Sacha decides that the civil marriage will be in Brussels.

September 22, 1933: After arriving, we visited Baron Charles Buxhoeveden and his daughter, the Baroness Elizabeth Buxhoeveden, well known in the annals of the revolution. She was the maid of honor in the marriage of Czar of Nicholas. She divides her time between Belgium and England. The house on Belliard Street is like a museum. Souvenirs of Russia and some of the countries where he was Ambassador in Sweden. We were all well received. September 23: We gathered before mid-day at the town hall of the Saint Gilles of Brussels. Receiving a first class reception with a red carpet and flowers, we met the mayor who was charming and full of compliments of Sacha. He marveled at Sacha's exploits in the war and decorations and for my father who was a fallen hero, which will be marked on the record of marriage. After the witnesses' signatures, we returned back to the hotel for a small banquet. After lunch, the Baron retires and the Gardines take us out for a tour of Brussels to Cambre Forest, then to the College of Saint Michael where the statue of Saint Gudule is. Sacha walks by me telling me sweet things. 'Am I dreaming?' I ask myself. Sacha left me at the door upon returning to Paris the same evening, as tomorrow we'd truly be married.

Wedding Day

September 24, 1933: It rained. The ceremony was set for two in the afternoon. My dress was a satin crepe with a long train and sleeves. I wore white gloves and a Russian style tiara of pearls and a large tulle veil. The maids of honor wore turquoise and black velvet. Two of the men of honor arrived with my wedding bouquet. We were late. Finally arriving at Daru Street at the Russian Church, we saw grandfather in his black frock coat and striped pants, top hat, and white gloves. He looked well. Taking my arm to walk down the aisle he appeared solemn and moved. Sacha was standing near the aisle dressed with his decorations. The maids of honor held my train as the music began. We drank wine from a silver goblet and carried out lit candles. The men of honor held crowns of gold above our heads. The priest took our hands, covering them with an ancient piece of silk, and walked us around the church. Following were the men with the crowns. In order to begin, we were stopped on a small rug in front of the aisle. It was an old custom that the first to place a foot down on the carpet would be master in the marriage. I let my future husband do the honor as we exchanged rings and the old priest spoke sweetly, telling us too embrace. The rain stopped as we posed seriously for the pictures. Then, my husband started laughing, causing me to laugh. We were truly happy. The reception was held at the Hotel de Paris and was very nice. A small band played discreetly the dances we loved. There were a few intimate friends and family and some grandfather did not want to see. We had the typical bigot family member show, but I danced with everyone and even grandfather, who did well. Then, gliding towards the exit I was to make my goodbyes to grandfather. I was completely taken as I hugged him and he uncontrollably began to cry. I consoled him with the misgiving that I would not see him again. I realized I had a tiny place in his heart after all. In the next room Paulette helped me change for my travels. She would take my gown for me. "Paulette," I said to her, "you must come to Nice as early as possible."

We left for the station Gare de Lyons to catch the night train for the Cote D'Azur. Sad to leave my family behind, my wedding night passed in the coach on wheels. Sacha sensed my sadness. The first scent of mimosas woke me in the morning. We arrived in a taxi. The governess awaited us on the steps. Then Sacha's mother, a very old lady in a lace bonnet, congratulated us. The villa was immense, more like a palace. It had been constructed for the Prince of Belgium. The following days, I would become more acquainted with my new home. Although the villa was lacking a woman's touch, there in our bedroom was the bed we bought in Paris. We never went to Italy as a business problem arose. Sacha's gardener and manger took off with a woman in Italy and money was missing. Sacha had to find a new manager of the villa as each day cost him money. People who bought apartments here wanted to move in on time. So, we went to the lake and it was just the way it seemed to be. End of November: It is certain that I am pregnant. I needed more time to organize the villa and pay the bills, so the news was not the best timing. Sacha was building another building in Cannes, so our funds were still low. I asked to have money for the house, bought an account book, and made a very modest budget thus succeeding in turning a corner. Sacha would often recount saying, "If I knew you ten years ago, we would be millionaires today!"

After many hard years, humanity had become ugly. One time recounted during all the craziness was on July 18, 1941. Their chateau was empty due to the war and, separating everyone out again, we stayed at a hotel. There we met an old Russian General Lipovath. His mother still lived in Rome as she was a Montenegrin, parent to the Queen of Italy. The general is charming as a Russian general can be. We speak of Paris where he lived, having been married to a French woman. That night, at dinner he invited an entire Tyrollian band, a countess living in Bolzano, a young Yogoslav, a German Baron who's mother was American, and an Austrian Baron — all disliked Hitler. They were all lovely and we had a good time. November 13: News came that the General Lipovitz was dead. November 1942: Life was becoming expensive and food scarce. Only with lots of money could it be found. It was bad for most people and, with us, terrible as we were a large family. When Christmas came, I was always sad as I thought of the ravages of war and the poor prisoners in those camps. March 30: Easter is upon us and I often read, "The Life of Jesus" by Maurice. He has a marvelous style, powerful with an emphasis on the truth, but all men that want to translate the Divine Word risk being inaccurate. End of May: We had to sell the villa and I thought to myself it is necessary to begin again. It was sold to a rich arms merchant from Genes who wanted it for his family because of future bombings. September 2: We have moved again in a villa that Sacha loves. I like it, but I found it too big and it's costly to heat the rooms. Food is more and more difficult to find. Turning thirty (years old) and what had I done? Had babies, moved, and had money worries. The mail is silent — nothing is in from France, Finland or America. November 11: Anniversary of the Armistice of 1918. But we are always fighting. Now it is in Morocco and Algeria, where the English and American forces fought Romel. When would this end? Turning once again to reading, I read that Charles Peguy was to have said to Joan of Arc, "The greatest in which has fallen on the world is the sin of despair!" Therefore, hope. I reread the Divine 'Marcus Aurelius.' Brief, he said, is life, and mine is nearly achieved and you do not respect yourself because you put your happiness in the soul of others. But how not to put one's well being in the souls of others? I only lived for others. And what joy [there is] in being in perfect union with the soul and thoughts of loved ones. September 5: Sacha is ill for the first time in our marriage.

September 10: The furious Germans had already occupied Genoa, Milan, Bologne, Venice, and Rome where they're marching on to Florence. Before this, parachutists had delivered Mussolini to prison. Things change as the war continues. September 24: Ten years of marriage and Father John of the Russian Church came for lunch giving us his blessing. September 25: We had our bombardment, English no doubt. Sacha was on the terrace with one of the children. We had not gone to the cellar, but there were victims and the next time we would need to go down below. October 5: Daily bombings with the German occupation. We used old draperies at home to make winter clothes for the children. Winter of 1943-44: Our cellar was ready for refuge and established publicly for the neighbors. The S.S. had their general headquarters not far from us. The town is occupied by German police. Rome is declared an open city and bombed despite the appeals of the Holy Father. We couldn't get Swiss radio as it was too dangerous. April 5, 1944: Sacha's brother was dead. Their apartment in Helsinki was bombed. April 22: The bombing of Paris and France continues, Roens is demolished, and the Cathedral attacked. It was the great battle of Monte Cassino. It was asked that if this Citadel was destroyed, what would become of the rest of Europe? July 21: The canons thundered all day long. Near us the battle raged on. The Allies approached us. The villas emptied at the same time. July 23: Another detachment of German soldiers occupied part of the village. The officer was lodged on the second floor. They moved in. The garden was transformed into a military parking lot. I believe in premonitions and the reality of some dreams. At the end of summer, I had a dream: We were alone in the villa and we were hunted and our belongings were to be stolen. We feared we were to be killed. It was so real that I persuaded my husband to hide some family objects of value. They were moved to a friend who was the consul of Romania. The second dream I had was at the beginning of the war. I had a vision of being etheric, seeming that Christ looked at me with such sad eyes and showing me streams of blood. I knew my husband was ill and that he would pass. I had dreamt this. We walked in the country where wild flowers were all about in the springtime. Then we arrived at a spot in the field and he disappeared. I couldn't go after him because there was a barrier in front of me. He himself, had a dream before his passing. Sacha dreamt of telling me, "When spring comes, my cares will end."

July 31: The Germans had left, but were replaced by others who called themselves I believe, 'The Destroyers.' They frightened me, but they only stayed for two days. They carried out our trunks, coverlets and some of our provisions. We are now without gas, electricity or water. We cooked with wood. The Allies approached, but the rumors were spreading and without radio, it was hard to tell what was what. We have been reduced to the stone age. August 2: We now retain two rooms in a hotel in the center of town. This morning the state of siege was declared. We could not leave. No one was allowed in the street except the doctors, priests or police. We were abandoned here as I had foreseen in my dream. Around two a.m. we were awakened by a violent explosion. The house shook and objects fell in the darkness. I stumbled on things looking for matches. We ran to the children and, by the grace of God, they were only frightened and not hurt. The Germans (The Destroyers) had been made to destroy the bridges on the Arno and the Rosso Point, which crossed the river close to us. On the second story the platform of the bathroom was broken and a door off its hinge. Windows were shattered everywhere. In the destroyed bathroom, the only thing remaining intact was a porcelain ashtray like some delicate vase. August 4: We are alone now. All the villas are empty. We pass the nights in the cellar. The English and Germans fight near us. We are between two forces as the shells travel past the villas. I had a premonition one day of being outside in the garden with the children. There was an explosion and one of the children brought a splinter from it, still warm. The child said, "You've escaped, it is fallen where you were seated!" We are protected I thought. Evidently I have always had great faith. A bomb crashed through our roof, rolled from the attic and [landed] on the first floor where we were. The halls were full of dust and we saw nothing. I put the children against the wall expecting the worst. If it went off, we were lost. Sacha, with his usual courage, went to go take a look. Our son was on top of his heels as he was Sacha's shadow. The bomb was found and it never went off. Later on, Italian partisans began arriving, traveling throughout he villa occupying the old place of the S.S. Later on more arrived wearing a red scarf with a communist emblem. They invaded the villa. They asked us if we had arms — now, Sacha always had a gun since France as he had a permit and fortunately hid it with my jewelry. It was announced we'd all be shot beginning with the children if we did not cooperate. Finding nothing, they gave us ten minutes to leave as three of them followed us with their guns aimed at our backs.

We went through our clothes hastily, taking our passports, papers and blankets. We found refuge with other partisans, not communists. There we spent the night with the children rolled up in the blankets on the ground. Sacha and I couldn't sleep. During the night, Sacha spoke with the Captain in charge about getting our gun and jewelry. Together, they went back to the villa as the invaders took over the place. Drank and ate our food, lying everywhere. They were asleep and didn't notice the Captain and Sacha. Our things were found and returned. In the morning we left for the center of town where not a soul was on the Via Bolognese's, which was mined. We risked our lives as Sacha took the lead, one after another in a straight line. One foot after the other... the poor children could have died of fear alone. But, they followed the line Sacha created and we arrived at Place Cavour, which was not mined. I prayed in thanks that day. At the hotel, they thought they had seen ghosts when we arrived. We were protected from unseen forces. Soon after we returned to the Hotel Baglioni, where we once again had to leave for the troops. They were everywhere, more than the Germans were. A small detachment of the 'pieds noirs' was commanded by a Captain and sergeant first passed Arno opening the French Consulate. The flag was put up. Once Sacha did not return for a long time and I became worried. When he did return, he said he had been stopped. An imbecile woman shouted that he was a German officer in civilian clothes, which led him to the secret police. Fortunately a young Russian Prince, Obolensky, recognized him and could identify him. One morning the bell rang and two men grabbed Sacha, ordering him to follow them to the perfecture for interrogation. I insisted on going with him and waited all day and night with Father John by my side as they had us get out of the car and they drove off. He was transferred to a camp with other foreigners like German Princes, bankers, a Czechoslovakian Count, Hungarians — all very good people. But the English weren't taking any chances. No word after that for a long time. The French Consulate re-opened. The Vice Consul helped me come back to the villa. What horror was left in that house from the English troops. My bed was still intact and we all slept in it. Sometimes I would be followed by drunken soldiers. Once I whacked one on the head with my umbrella as he fell down and passed out. One night a man came secretly telling us that our families were being moved to an English camp. 'Bring what you can,' he said. I thanked the man and paced the vestibule praying as the little ones slept. There on a chair, was Sacha's overcoat rolled up in a ball. I was surprised. I opened it up and there was a letter of encouragement and money. Half my prayer had been answered.

The next day we went to the prison, but I could not see Sacha without permission. From this moment on, I went to the English secret police to obtain the address of the camp each day. We would have to wait in a small room for hours to do this. One day I refused to leave and I was led [away] by a rude and arrogant officer with no results. Since then, he received me well and we began to speak. He told me of the time that imprisoned foreigners were killed very easily by the Italians. They had proved nothing against Sacha. Soviet Russia was their great ally and for this the White Russians were their enemy. More then once I begged for him to take a letter to Sacha. Then I stopped going there. One morning I was called to their office. It was a proposed to me that I work for them spying. I listened to every word. The payment was freedom for my husband. I was no longer mad. I told them I was not a spy for the English or the Italians and that my husband had done nothing. They must free him with blackmail. He was later liberated, one of the first at the armistice. We found another apartment, which was another miracle. We moved to the other side of town, to 'Poggio Imperial.' One afternoon I was approached by a man who slipped me a letter. I recognized the handwriting right away. Sacha asked me to respond back the same way. The internees had found this means of communication with their families by the intermediary of the barber who cut the men's hair. This shrewd Neapolitan barber like the 'Figaro de Beaumarchais' took the letters and hid them in the soles of his shoes. All this under the noses of the English. I liked the small apartment and the boys went to Catholic school. The girls went to a pension with Belgian sisters. There I knew they'd be safe and have a regular life. As Allied subjects, the children and I had the right to American food at a reasonable price because food was still hard to find. We began to live again.

After the War

I am sick… all is somber. The sickness is an invasion of the reality. Each of us has the right to eternal life. Days passed with the venetian blinds shut as if one could ever forget. In a dream I went to a place to forget and I went back to my past life and thought of George. I saw him, thin and dark haired. Soft black eyes and a beautiful smile. His favorite poem to me was "Reversibilite" by Baudelaire. Back to reality, will we leave for the new world? Sacha is disgusted with Europe and its continual revolutions. He returned from the camp thin and not in good health. He needs a change. He wants to rejoin his son in New York. What I knew of America was from gangster or cowboy films and didn't inspire me much. I am sure there is a more spiritual life to discover. Once again, I was pregnant. We sell some of our things and go to the American Consulate at Genoa. Saying goodbye to some friends, we make the trip aboard The Volcana in the month of July 1946. When I boarded the ship many thoughts ran through my mind. My step-son married a woman who went through several divorces and was much older. Sacha's never approved, but I tried to be amicable to her just the same. She leads Sacha's son by the nose. How are we going to find ourselves? When the Italian land disappeared before my eyes, tears came to me. Would I ever be back? I was leaving the struggles and those dearest to me behind. Paulette remained in France with her husband and they would never set foot outside the country. The voyage was awful; sea storms and everyone was sick. Except for Sacha who walked around everywhere, dining alone in the room with all the servers [waiting on] him.

After a week of sailing, we arrived in New York. At debarkation, Sacha's son and his 'charming' wife, Vera, meet us. After all the immigration formalities were finished we left in their car. We arrived on Long Island, where the homes appeared minuscule, like doll houses. After the palaces of Italy, it was a change to understand. For awhile Sacha's son's wife was nice, but it didn't last long. We perceived that all that they wanted was to win the suit against the Estonian Bank of which part of the funds were frozen by the American government. We were living in a room in their home and the children occupied the attic. We paid them, but it was clear we were not wanted. Sacha often went to the city for business matters. He spoke English well and did well. But, the competition and lack of experience in the new world did not help him. September: Daniel was born and thank God in good health. I was alone in the maternity ward and I had no one to visit. The nurses and doctors were not as friendly as those in Europe. Poor Sacha came to see me, but he had all the worries of the children and preparing meals and school. On one visit, he brought bad news. [The previous] Saturday he took the children to the cinema and then they went to play with some friends. When they were going up the road to the house, a policeman was waiting with the children. The house was closed. He learned that the children, upon returning around 6 p.m., found the house locked, so our oldest son went for help. The police helped find friends of the Buxhoevedens and make them come back and open up the house. I had to return to this with a newborn in this already poisoned atmosphere. How can anyone be so evil?

May, 1948: It was too much for Sacha. He had a stroke and was partially paralyzed and unable to talk. His last days were spent in the hospital at the insistence of his son's evil wife and the doctors. I wanted him near me until it was time. He couldn't speak to me, but his hand held mine until the end. During this time, the children caught the mumps and I had to isolate the baby. I had no one but my older son to help me. The poor child had already been through so much. He found money for medicine and milk for the baby. He took care of it. May 13: The funeral was a dream I was walking into. After the Orthodox service, the candles we lit set my veil on fire! We went to an area in Queens, where we buried Sacha in the rain — we married in the rain and he departed into the ground in the rain. I tried to go over in my mind the beautiful memories and that dream I had not so long ago. "When the spring comes, I will no longer have worries."

Catherine on her father

"Mother told me that I was close to my father and that he loved me very much. During the war in Italy, we moved so many times. My father was arrested by the English forces, mother having four children to care for, placing Rosemarie and I in the nunnery for safe keeping, shelter and food in Florence. I was four years old and Rosemarie a little over five. We stayed there for one year and did not see my father for a long time. At some point after that, mother was able to procure an apartment in Florence in the anticipation of my father's release. We all moved there and father was to come home for Easter, but did not make it until much later. I remember in Great Neck, Long Island, when he had had a stroke and was in bed paralyzed on one side, spending time with him. I was also helping mother with my brother Danny, who was only a few months old then. I slept in their room, which was above the garage. During my childhood, some things I can't remember while others stayed with me, like, in order to keep pants pressed, they put them under the mattress! We used newspaper for toilet paper and on it goes. When father died, for many years I dreamed that he had come back and thought about him often. On this day as I write this, May 11, I automatically recall his passing."

Reflection

All throughout Rosine's life, she prayed and her prayers were answered. She went on to marry a German man and gave the children a second father. She would continue to struggle as they moved around Long Island a couple of more times settling in Ronkonkoma. A new hope for the new future. Fate dealt this family many blows as it did many solutions and they all grew older, creating lives of their own. The children, now adults, would have to also go through many turbulences, but were the wiser for it and were given opportunities in America where there was freedom. The oldest son was stationed in Japan, the next went to join an Orthodox Russian monastery in Jordanville, New York. The youngest son was admitted to Girard College in Philadelphia, which was founded by a Frenchman named Stephen Girard in 1882 for orphaned males of the white race of French origin. The girls finished their studies, becoming young ladies. Rosine went to work with her step-son in the decorating business, opening up a store in Great Neck. Sacha's son had divorced and would often visit Rosine for lunch as well. Her new marriage to the German man was another blessing and he loved the children dearly. She would go on and share twenty years of her life with this man named Hans Kessler. He was born in Sarre and joined the army at eighteen years of age. Not understanding why he should fight the French, he didn't. He was very logical. Part of his heritage came from Greek culture. He would refer to the television and radio as 'music in a box.' He didn't like food from a box either. Having done his studies at Bonn University he became a disciple of Rudolph Steiner, the last founder of the anthropoid movement. He followed him to Switzerland to the 'Goethanum Dornach.' Steiner was a precursor in certain scientific and spiritual education, organic cultivation, and an educator of mentally challenged children. After his stay in Vienna, he lectured these philosophies around the country. He spoke to miners who suffered many horrible conditions with their work. Later, he opened a school for mentally challenged children with two of his colleagues. He founded a newspaper, which was a weekly publication. Writing articles with his colleagues, one paper was titled, "The Turning of Civilization." Before meeting Rosine, he had met the spiritual writer, Harold Percival, who wrote the impressive work, "Thinking and Destiny." Hans would comment that there were many differences in America, one being the difference of the multiplicity of religions. There were all sorts from Christianity to Paganism. At least people had the right to think what they wanted, which was good. On this great continent, everything is immense. The giant trees in California, the Canadian forests several centuries old, and so on. In contrast, there is poison ivy, poison sumac infecting your skin. Legend says that Indians threw something on these plants against the whites because they, themselves, were immune. In 1959, Hans and Rosine moved to Lake Ronkonkoma where they would stay until his passing. All the children made their lives in different fashions.

December, 1965: "The police rang our door bell. I didn't understand what they wanted to say, then finally realized... my eldest son had been killed in an automobile accident returning from Chicago that very night. I was overwhelmed by this revelation and not able to cry. I thought of his six-month old baby and two-year old daughter. Months passed. Now, as the youngest, Daniel knows the horrors of war. Making the long trip across the United States, we went to see him in Colorado, where they were training the young soldiers. He was first sent to Korea then Vietnam. He did return home, but only with psychological scars. When he lived with us, he was often sad. But, when he became a pilot, flying became his joy." Rosine battles her own health issues with beniegn brain tumors and slowly recoups her memory. 1978: Hans (Kessler) would show the first signs of his illness. He succumbs to cancer in October of that year.

Taking his hand in the end once again as she had done with Sacha, watched as the imprisoned soul flew away with the last breath.

Catherine on Hans Kessler

"He influenced mother on how she should act towards her children as mother acquiesced to men, which is the culture and times she came from. She made it known that she prefers having boys then girls, which were made with hints and innuendoes. I believe it was Hans that made my sister leave home and then myself right after graduating high school. I don't know what their relationship was, but I got along with him for the most part because of mother. I know he liked me because I was intelligent, capable and a doer, and he could talk to me. He would always tell me that. There is a very good saying: "We are not put on this earth to live up to people's expectations."

Chapter Twenty-One:

AT DEATH'S DOOR

Rosine settled on Long Island, but moved around for years. After her second husband passed from cancer, she stayed. Her children Catherine, Rosemarie and Daniel Buxhoeveden tried to help her stay independent. After two wars, two husbands dying terrible deaths, and five children, she really needed to keep her identity going. So the family always supported her way of life not depending on anyone. But I still felt very sad for her after all her losses. She had lost my late Uncle Theodore, adoringly nicknamed Teddy, to a horrible car accident. Falling asleep in his car after work on a bridge, Teddy's car was struck by another vehicle and he and the car plummeted off the bridge. He had been on leave from the Army for only a short while when it happened. I remember as a teenager asking Rosine about Uncle Teddy's death. She said it was in the papers, but she couldn't bear to look. She tossed it out and never looked back again. But, the strong Parisian that she was, continued on with the four remaining children from the Count.

Of course tragedy would strike her again as her other son, Alex, who had been born with a slight mental disability, disowned Rosine, spreading lies about her to anyone who would listen. He married a much older woman who hoarded his money and told him how to breath and everything else. He couldn't wipe his ass without her permission. He ended up getting a part time computer job, as his wife was the one mothering him. It broke Rosine's heart into a million pieces, but again, she and the rest of the family moved on and let him be. It wouldn't be until my late Aunt Rosemarie's funeral that this pain would come back. Rosemarie was the one with whom I communicated with two years after her passing. She is the sole reason I am writing today and will continue to write. Rosemarie was diagnosed with a rare form of Lymphoma that began growing on the outside of her lower leg. She was given six weeks to live unless she underwent radical treatments, hence increasing her life expectancy up to two years. She told no one of this other than her husband, and her closest dear spiritual friend. At that time, Catherine and Daniel moved Rosine into Rosemarie and Tony's home in Queens to help her out. Catherine had already taken in Rosine and Daniel lived too far away, so Rosemarie was next in line and offered graciously to have 'mother' as they affectionally referred to her as. Time passed. Then, during a ride up to my home in Upstate New York, Rosemarie leaned into Catherine while she was driving and said, "Cathy, I have to tell you something." Catherine listened to what was going to be the next family tragedy. Rosemarie calmly and pleasantly said, "I have cancer."

Of course knowing how Rosemarie was with her way and words, she told it like telling a story to a child with great enthusiasm and hope of a happy ending. But, this was not the case and none of us knew until two weeks before she died, that she was dying. The whole two years passed and it wouldn't be until my phone call one day that outed the whole cover up. I placed my weekly call to Rosemarie checking in on how she felt after her treatments, and it was Uncle Tony who had answered the phone. He sounded weak, frazzled and saddened. When I asked to speak with my aunt, he broke down and cried. He said she was no longer able to walk to the phone, and he had to move her to the couch. He cried to my aunt telling her that it was I on the phone. Seconds later after sniffling, he said that Rosemarie said to tell me she loves me. I lost it. Every ounce of my being melted away onto my floor as there was no one to pick me back up. I didn't understand. How could this be? She said she was fine, he said she was fine. Then, I made the round of calls, playing operator and soon it was known the end was near. At the funeral service in Queens, after decades of a grand disappearing act, my Uncle Alexander showed up. My heart stopped. I quickly grabbed my sister and rushed to Rosine's side. At the time, I had two small children who were out in the entranceway with their father. My third child, six weeks old, was being held in the room by my father-in-law and his wife who sadly was diagnosed with cancer as well. It was an odd mix of emotional depth that morning.

My Uncle Alex stood very tall and slender. His hair was black like mine, but had grayed over the years. His face remained the same, so did his deep muddled voice. Rosine had shrunk over the years, so he really towered over her now. He spoke with a slur as his speech was poor and rushed. Rosine looked up into her son's eyes as if for the first time. Hurt, betrayed and bitter, during that moment it was put aside if not just to remember the son she gave birth too. I had also posed the question to her as a child on how did Uncle Alex end up the way he did? Rosine told me that at the time of her pregnancy with Alex, she had to have emergency surgery due to appendicitis. No one knew including herself that she was with child. The drugs and trauma to her body caused Alex's birth defect. At the funeral, Alex was excitable and happy to see everyone. He loved seeing my babies, as he was childlike himself.

When I was a child, he'd come over and throw me up in the air. Once I thought I was going through that concrete ceiling for sure! I remember Hans and Catherine nervously saying, "Shushuk, put her down, please." I went to embrace him and what do you think he did? Well, he certainly didn't throw me anywhere, but he lifted me off the ground. Now I found myself saying to him, "Shushuk, please put me down." Rosine had him bend down so she could fix his hair and pat his face. I could see the tears well up in her eyes. My heart broke again that day. I tried a decade ago to call him and get him to stop the nonsense, but it didn't work. Rosemarie sometimes would visit him after work in the city and give him some money. She was always doing that. Even my cousin tried to help him, but that only got him into potential legal trouble as Alex went back to his lying, ranting ways. Now no one has any contact with him other than perhaps Uncle Tony. But even that is few and far, as he finally was able to begin a new life after three years. Poor Rosine had lost again.

Now, left with two children out of five and no more spouses, she is left to live out the rest of her life with those thoughts and impressions. Sometimes Rosine would reminisce about the Count and their days together. She'd also do that about her second husband, Hans Kessler, who was the only grandfather Nadine and I ever knew. Hans' father Leo passed when Nadine was a baby.

In the end, it is our family regardless how big or small that matters. Some aren't as lucky as others with being blessed or surrounded by good souls, so it may come in the form of friends. But whichever form, cherish those as they age and we are all living on borrowed time.

Ironically, it is Grandpa Leo who visited Hans in the hospital some years back during a terrifying moment. Hans had surgery on his leg and slipped into a bit of panic mode. He had walking pneumonia and didn't know it. He had tripped in his office lair and broke his leg bone. He never understood how he fell. I told him, "I know." When Hans asked how, I explained, "Rosemarie told me she had to trip you so you'd go to the hospital because you were sick in your lungs. And knowing you, you'd never go in time." When Hans was gripping on to his life at 3 a.m., as I got the call from his doctor, my heart broke yet again. I prayed even harder that time. Later on I began communication with Grandpa Leo as Rosemarie faded back and left. When I told this to Hans and described his father, he laughed. He told me of the visit he had with his father the night he could have passed in that hospital. Leo said he was there to check in and that it wasn't his time and then Leo left. The doctors thought Hans was crazy and it was part of his trauma. Which is very realistic, but when it comes to the ghost hunter, highly unlikely. They all loved him there, as he gave them free readings and books.

Chapter Twenty-Two:

Final Q&A's:
Perspective of a Ghost Hunter
A.K.A Professor Paranormal

These last two question and answer interviews are some of the best I have read and would like to expose them further. The first article really is meant to explain that some individuals may feel people, such as Hans, are a bit off or not on the same page. Who isn't? We are all a bit off to some degree. The question is just how much and how bad. Hans always had it under control, as he knew the ghost business inside and out. I don't believe there are many who can challenge him and, long after he is gone, his will be a hard path to follow.

By Barry Shlachter, *Associated Press*: The Austrian born New Yorker makes a living writing and lecturing on his experiences tracking down ghosts, discarnates and apparitions, and ridding homes of them. Holzer said that after writing a 1963 book, one of eighty-five, called *Ghost Hunter*, he registered the title as a trademark, but now is uncomfortable with the label.

> Hans: I find it embarrassing and I've been trying to shake it ever since. Then along comes a film, 'Ghost Busters,' which I hate, because it's funny and we're serious people. We're not nuts.

I mentioned this mere fact. It's funny how he and I make the same correlation. Great minds think alike? Well, I'd like to think so. This article was written twenty years ago and it reads like some of the more recent ones, which proves my belief that Hans sticks to his guns.

Reporter: Holzer, 66, charges nothing for locating and later persuading ghosts to leave a person's home. But, deluged with requests, he now only accepts assignments that pose an interesting "scientific case or when a person is truly troubled" by the spirits of the not so departed. "Ghosts," he explains, "are people who die suddenly or after long suffering and in shocking conditions and are unaware of their own deaths. They haven't gone any place because they are like psychotics without a body." He calls them "stay behinds." But there aren't that many.

Hans: Only a tiny percentage of people don't go normally to the next phase of existence. They are the exception rather than the rule.

Reporter: But in all his years on their trail, ghosts have never made themselves visible to Holzer and that makes no difference to him.

Hans: I am not interested in seeing a ghost. Does a doctor have to be sick in order to be a doctor? It's a stupid question. I am an investigator. I am writer. I am not medium.

Reporter: Scholars around the country have yet to find evidence of psychic phenomena that can withstand scientific scrutiny. Psychology Professor Donald McBurney, of the University of Pittsburgh, one of a dozen scholars and magicians who investigate purported communication with ghosts and alleged cases of other psychic talents, said Holzer's findings represent "unsubstantiated claims. They would not pass scientific muster. Holzer is one of the prominent ghost hunters and these people generally avoid us like a plague." During the past three years, McBurney's Paranormal Investigating Committee of Pittsburgh has offered Holzer and others a $10,000 prize if they can prove their boasts. Holzer has yet to take up the challenge, and as for the more than one hundred who have, "we have yet to find any evidence for any paranormal claim." Holzer says that laboratory experiments prove nothing.

Hans: We all know volcanoes erupt, but we can't reproduce them in a laboratory. We are talking about scientific observation en masse, and conclusions drawn from that.

Reporter: Over the years, he personally has gathered loads of evidence by interviewing thousands who have come face to face with ghosts, he said. He has written up what he found in stories his publisher, Yankee Books of Dublin, New Hampshire, calls "spine-tingling encounters." Last month, it reissued his 1966 book, *Yankee Ghosts*, about discarnate New Englanders.

Hans: The *Yankee Ghosts* show the same remarkable individuality and sense of moral fiber as their living counterparts. But with ghosts of any stripe, you have to be firm.

Reporter: When one refuses to leave a family alone, Holzer responds with a "rescue circle" that employs a spiritual medium who makes contact with the disturbed person called a ghost and you gently reason with him by explaining the true status of his house, that time has passed.

Hans: I am very much like a psychoanalyst, but my patient is not on a couch… it is within the body of an unconscious trans medium — temporarily.

Next Q&A Interview. By now, if you haven't gotten an incredible description of what a ghost is, then I am at a loss for words and that would be scary! Most interviews begin with the next sentence, "He is the author of over one hundred books dealing with the Paranormal and Parapsychology." And why not. It is quite an accomplishment and so it is only fitting. I would be so lucky. "He studied at the University of Vienna, graduated the Academy of Vienna and received his PhD in Parapsychology at the London College of Applied Science. It's a rare honor indeed to present an interview with Dr. Hans Holzer, "Professor of Paranormal."

Next is a great session that touches on some newer mediums. Not new to the media as much as to his generation. Some may take offense to his comments, but everyone is entitled to their opinion and, he included, has had many remarks made about him in a negative way. When you put yourself out there, it's for the taking in the form of freedom of speech. I too, will be joining those ranks and will need an extra layer of skin, cases of wine and hair dye!

Q: I guess I should start off by asking if you still write books these days. **A**: Oh, yeah, but I'm now also involved with my film projects. I have nine screenplays, not all on the paranormal, some are comedies. I also do plays, theatrical plays and musicals. I do all of those, and I'm currently trying to get producers!

Q: Would any of your books on the paranormal make it to the Silver Screen? **A**: I've written about the paranormal, all non-fiction of course. But, I've also written some movies, some screen-plays, on paranormal things, but fictional. Authentic stuff, but still fictional. I have a film script called 'The Psychics.' She knows everybody's future but her own. It deals with a fictional psychic whose boyfriend is a detective and she somehow becomes famous with the mob. They like her predictions and unfortunately she finds out too much. There's of course a double-ending. She's in trouble, but, she doesn't get killed after all. I admire Agatha Christie a great deal. I think she's wonderful. I write things of that kind. That's fiction of course. I do as much fiction as I do non-fiction. You don't fool around. You just tell it like it is journalistically. With fiction you can do other things.

Q: Your definition of a ghost is, "People who have unfinished business on their minds when they passed on." Is it possible that when they re-build the World Trade Center, people will go out into the hallway and smell smoke or hear screams? I guess what I'm asking is, are those grounds haunted? **A**: We all have the potential of being psychic that is receptive. Some more, some less. If there are some people that are very psychic, they will of course see it or feel it. Nobody has been down there to put at rest the ones who died there. There are some people who died there I'm sure who are confused about what happened, and they need help. But, I can't do it. Ghosts are generally not aware that they're dead, as a result of which there's a lot of confusion, a lot of trapped people. I don't say souls, because I don't have any use for religion. But, they are trapped individuals, personalities who need help.

Q: Would the property where the Oklahoma City bombing took place be haunted as well? **A**: Of course. Whenever someone is surprised by sudden death and not prepared for it obviously chances are they don't realize they've passed on. If somebody is psychic enough, they may make contact with them if they are professional trans mediums. But, the average person is not that powerful. Never-the-less they will pick it up, sure.

Q: If a medium went to 875 Bundy Drive in Los Angeles, could that person contact the spirit of Nicole Brown Simpson and Ron Goldman and find out exactly what happened to them? **A**: If this is a deep Trans Medium, which is much more powerful, getting out of their own body to let the other entity get in and speak, yeah. That is how it works, sure. I've done work like that for the police; cases where we had an object that belonged to the murdered person. I had a very good Trans Medium with me. This was Sybil Leek if I'm not mistaken. They spoke to her and named somebody and the police followed up, because I was with the police officer there. They got him. That does happen from time to time, yeah.

Q: Have you ever seen Sylvia Browne or John Edwards on TV? **A**: Sylvia Browne, I have never talked to. I understand she has some gift. It's a natural gift. But, I don't like the way she promotes herself. Edwards, I see. I think if the audience were separated more from his readings, he wouldn't be able to pick things up directly. That's what I'm concerned about. Q: Do you believe then that both of these people are gifted in their chosen line of work? A: They are gifted. By the way I don't have the term belief, disbelief, supernatural in my vocabulary. I am not a religious person. I'm a spiritual person. I have no use for religion, organized or otherwise. I believe in living a spiritual way of life.

Q: You say that ghosts don't travel. Is that correct? **A**: Yes. Ghosts are not like spirits. Let me explain what we are made of: when we are born, we are born in a double body, which is derived from either parents or grandparents. It's called the Medallion Law. It's well known. But, from another source, those thinking of reincarnating again, the staff should we say, they're called the 'Beings of Light,' they will select an appropriate couple. Then you will have to walk to the well of forgetfulness they call it and you will be born again. This happens, but it's very carefully controlled by them. We have no way of deciding who we will be next time.

Q: On November 22, 1963, John F. Kennedy was killed in Dallas, Texas. Some people have said they've seen a young John Kennedy walking along the streets of Palm Beach, Florida. How is that possible? **A**: Oh, very simple. At the time of the elusion of the outer body, not the inner body, nearly everybody reverts back to their best years. They all look younger after death. If somebody has seen a younger Kennedy, that is normal. The only time the person will appear at the aged level is when they need to do this to be recognized, but generally they are reverting to their best years.

Q: It seems that not everyone can see a ghost or has seen a ghost. Is it possible to have seen a ghost and not know it? **A**: Well, first of all, the difference is to be made in three ways; ghosts and spirits are not the same. In my book Ghosts, which is now 150,000 or more in print and is a huge seller, and by the way Barnes and Noble is also publishing my older books again, which is a good thing for younger people who weren't around when I wrote them. There's one sure way to tell: if you see a spirit and you see the spirit again or somebody else sees the spirit in the same place, at the same time, more than once, chances are you are seeing an impression from the past. If there's any chance in how they appear, any chance in what they do they are individuals, but, if they always appear the same, if they always appear at the same place at the same time, those are imprints from the past, not people, not living people. We call them psychic imprints.

Q: You talk about imprints left behind in the atmosphere by an individuals passing. You say, "Anyone possessed of psychic ability will sense the event from the past." Something like that happened to me. **A**: Yeah, except it's not the atmosphere. It's the ether. The ether is part of the atmosphere but, it's the part of the atmosphere that is psychically loaded, so to speak. In the ether there are imprints from the past, which is a non-existent commodity. There is no time on the other side. Anybody who is gifted to that extent that they can pick up the imprint will tell you. That's why a lot of good mediums sometimes can't tell the difference whether what they pick up is really the person's spirit or an imprint from the past which has no life.

Q: Back in 1980, while en route to Washington, D.C. I got lost in Pennsylvania. I passed through an area, and immediately sensed something had happened there. I didn't see anything, but I felt something of importance happened in the area. Sure enough, the sign on the road said, "Gettysburg," and I was passing by a battlefield. **A**: Yeah. That is the meaning of psychic ability. That is very normal. People think that cemeteries are filled with ghosts. They're not. Once a person dies in the physical body, they're not there anymore. There's nobody there. Cemeteries are empty real estate. The minute they're out of the outer body, they're gone. That's why it's foolish to have cemeteries, but that's the way the world is.

Q: Let me run another story by you that happened to me a couple of years ago. I knew a girl who worked for a department store. One afternoon, a sunny afternoon in October, I happened to be driving past this store and saw this girl outside helping a customer load a box into their trunk. I had to look twice because surrounding this girl was what I would describe was white light, a white aura, so brilliant that I could actually see light bouncing off her. I thought it was the sun's reflection, but it wasn't. Two days later this girl was walking to work and she was hit by a car and died. What did I see surrounding this girl just two days prior, her aura? I had never seen anything like it before or since then for that matter. **A**: That's called distant vision. It doesn't necessarily have to do with dead people or with spirits or with ghosts. It's a normal human ability that some people have more of or less of. But, it does not necessarily have to be about dead people. Seeing the aura, the aura is the secondary body that is inside the outer body. You saw the aura. Now, have you ever seen the aura of a person who was not killed afterwards? **Q**: No. **A**: Well, you saw the aura when she was still alive. **Q**: Yes. **A**: The fact that she was killed later had nothing to do with it. **Q**: Someone told me the fact that I saw her surrounded by white light meant that she was at peace with herself. **A**: Well, that's religion. Religion preaches that, but it doesn't really hold true. Remember there are very many saints shown with a halo. Then there are those pretty girls with goose feathers on their back called angels. This is from the misinterpretation of the aura. What people saw was the aura. There are no angels with wings. There are no saints with halos. But, the aura sometimes extends beyond the physical body and some people can see it.

Q: Can personal pets come back to a place they've lived after their death? **A**: Animals are frequently very sensitive, very psychic. That's very common. Some animals more than others. Animals by and large are frequently sensitive, especially cats. Cats are extremely sensitive. They can read your mind in a way. For instance the cat I have is a beautiful black cat. She's twelve years old. When I call her by name, she comes. When I say sit down, she sits down. But that's because we have a very close relationship. There's nothing supernatural about that.

Q: When a person dies, will they come back to reside in the home they've known? **A**: First of all, they don't come back. They don't return from anywhere. They haven't gone yet. Secondly, when someone passes on, they will then be on the other side of life. Some people like to call it Heaven and Hell, but it's right here next door. Then they will be on the other side. Frequently, especially when they have been in the same place most of their lives, like an old woman who's used to her wheelchair, they will return to where they used to be. It happens particularly in hospitals. Hospitals are really not where they want to be. The next thing, they are dead and back home in their wheelchair or chair. That happens frequently. But remember, they are spirits. They are not ghosts. Ghosts are people who have passed frequently with unfinished business, but not always unfinished business. Sometimes they are just shocked by the fact that they are dead and they don't realize they're dead. That can also create a ghost. They don't travel. They are stuck in the place where it occurred. If you're in that spot, there's a chance you might feel it or see it, but they don't travel generally. Spirits on the other hand are free to go wherever they want. They can appear to you if they get permission. The other side is a bureaucracy just like this side. In order for somebody who's on the other side to communicate with you; first of all you have to get permission from the people who run the other side. They call themselves the Beings of Light. I got this from them. I got it from numerous cases of near death experiences. They always talk about the Beings of Light. They will have to get permission to make contact. If they get permission, there has to be a good reason for it, not just to find out where Uncle Frank put the money. They will ask permission for making contact. Then they have to find themselves, if they are not psychic themselves, a good medium to form the good contact. That's how it works." © Gary James, All Rights Reserved.

Chapter Twenty-Three:

Just the Facts, Ma'am!
An ode to Hans' Legacy and his wealth of paranormal knowledge

The following are random pieces taken from some of his books. It is a spiritual and ghostly dictionary easy to understand and digest. It is information Hans has discovered during his long career in this very controversial field. I hope to show you, the reader, how insightful and informative he was and still is. For his newer titles, aside from the latest Amityville book, which I will include a small snippet for all you Amity folks, they offer new insight and cemented information for the next generation of the unexplained. Through these explanations I hope to encourage discussion about topics that are fascinating whether one believes or not. Hans has written at least one thing in there that may sway even the skeptic in a positive manner. It isn't just about ghosts at the end of the day. It's about inner peace and were you a good soul. That is how Hans lived and still lives. A lesson some of us may learn after knowing more about the man deemed the original 'Ghost Hunter.' This is taken from his book, Are You Psychic?

The astral-physical connection: A human being is essentially a unique electromagnetic field, consisting of pure energy, temporarily housed in a denser layer of matter called the physical body. As long as a person is alive in the physical world, his or her astral body remains attached to its physical counterpart by a thin connecting link called the silver cord, a kind of cable through which impulses go back and forth. At the time of physical death, the cord is indeed severed and the astral body floats freely outward into the next dimension.

Out-of-body Experiences: The phenomena of out-of-body experiences and bilocation prove that we can function fully without the physical body. This is because there is within each of us a secondary body variously called the etheric body, aura, or soul, that is the true vehicle of the self. The movement of this inner body and all communications by and with it, are part of the dimension we call the astral, the etheric, or the psychic.

Near Death Experience: Perhaps the single most common thread in near-death experiences is the feeling of being at peace that seems to follow a feeling of serenity and contentment and, most notably, a complete absence of the fear of death. Upon their return, these travelers often seem to have undergone profound changes. Their attitudes toward life and death usually change completely, allowing them to live the rest of their lives with a feeling of being more at peace. In addition, in many cases, their inherent psychic ability is fully awakened, and to their amazement, they have become psychic. Apparently exposure to the next dimension, the *Other Side*, can trigger an increase in psychic ability. Some people are quick to argue that near-death experiences are nothing more than hallucinations, mental aberrations, or fantasies brought about by situations of extreme stress. I cannot emphasize strongly enough that authentic near death experiences do not fall into this category. The clarity of the experience, the full memory of it afterwards, and the many parallels between individual experiences reported by different people in widely scattered areas weigh heavily against the possibility that these experiences are of hallucinatory origin.

Reincarnation: Reincarnation is the return of the true self (or soul) after death to earthly existence in another life. Belief in reincarnation is common throughout the world, particularly in Asian cultures. In the Far East, reincarnation is widely accepted as a matter of fact because many Eastern religions have incorporated this concept into their belief systems. In Tibet, the idea of reincarnation has also been a practical way of government. Less well known are passages in the Bible that hint at the idea of reincarnation in Jewish culture. The concept of Karma holds that the object of existence is to achieve a certain level of perfection and that the soul makes a fresh start from incarnation to incarnation until this is achieved; at this point, no further return to a bodily existence is necessary. According to the classic idea of reincarnation, memories of one lifetime are supposed to be wiped out completely prior to the beginning of the next journey in the body. However, there seem to be a limited number of cases in which the system simply doesn't work as it should, and the result is a phenomenon called the reincarnation memory [through recurrent dreams or hypnotic regression] It appears that we all reincarnate, but the lengths between lives and the frequency of return may vary.

Dreams (*my favorite*): Much psychic material comes to the surface in dreams. This is because it's easier for such information to reach the mind when the mind is not otherwise occupied and is in a resting state.

Automatic Writing: Automatic writing is another phenomenon in which an external source communicates through a living person, but in this case using the written rather than the spoken word. The person attempting to serve as a channel of communication for a discarnate entity holds a pen or pencil and allows it to be guided by that entity. In addition to being guided, as it were, by an unseen hand, an automatic writer receives information and impulses to write down sentences faster than he or she ordinarily would be able to do so. One of the earmarks of genuine automatic writing is the tremendous speed in which dictation takes place.

Hypnosis (*this is excerpted from his book to show why you should read up on this topic*): Each of us has the power to dramatically change the way we live our lives. We can also use this power to subtly influence others. In our business dealings and social get-togethers, as well as in our personal relationships. Although most of us know of this power, few of us have the knowledge to use it. But those who understand its use can truly alter their destinies. It is hypnosis, the power to control the subconscious through post-hypnotic suggestion.

Have you ever wished to lose weight, give up smoking, quit biting your nails, or stop dozens of other bad habits? Have you ever wanted to become a better lover? Hypnosis can make it happen. In this easy to understand book, Dr. Holzer offers a fascinating look at the world of hypnosis. He begins by examining how this power is used in everyday life through advertising, politics, and other means. He then explains what hypnosis is and how it works, and provides basic dos and don'ts. From there, he explores the use of hypnosis in areas such as healing, stress reduction, love, and more. If you are looking for a way to overcome your fears, increase your willpower, and take charge of your life, the answer may be contained in this book. Whether self induced or performed by a professional, the power of hypnosis is real, effective, and ready to be tapped.

I can appreciate this introduction as it sends a positive message. It is important to include some of Hans' work in this memoir as it is the foundation to what he was and is meant to be. Hans as a person, spouse, father, paranormal investigator, great friend to all those he meets, a giver, a lover not a fighter, a ground breaker into the unknown, fearless and the list goes on. This is probably why they don't want him in heaven. He really would try and take over.

WHERE THE HOLZERS ARE TODAY

Thoughts and Honest Feelings

Catherine: She would like those reading to know her side of the marriage: "He was a good husband, very kind, and appreciated my talents, which were and are many, supporting me in my art work. (I have always painted, in most cases with literally no space, always in a corner of a room.) I am interested in music, theater and all the arts. Hans wanted me to work with him on the Parapsychology Investigation work, which I did, which is when we came up with the idea of doing the book cover illustrations. The art world had just started exploring pen and ink drawings. All this went on until the mid 1970s, when the 'wind shifted' in the book industry and the paranormal subject. Hans could have been more successful had he not wanted to have things done his way at most times. He believed what people told him in business — he is not a business person, and did not understand how to play the 'game' to make it happen — and had no sense of money. Hans is extremely sensitive and very insecure of his person and he would not listen to me; he knew best. He manipulates and I know indirectly that he has borrowed money from different people that has never been paid back. He got into trouble with the IRS, which caused them to take thousands from my account to pay for New York State taxes.

1961, Catherine and Hans at first Artist & Models Ball. Hans was artistic director and Catherine was on the committee.

The IRS payback was ongoing and I had been working and saving to divorce him. I knew there would be no 'support' paid, so I obtained my own attorney. He refused to move to another apartment, which I was happy to help with etc. as I wanted to stay with Alex and Nadine, especially Alex, since she was still in school. He left me no choice and so began my life moving around again.

Hans could have pursued it further with an attorney, but did not want to do that. I wanted an amicable divorce and so did he. Fundamentally, Hans was a wonderful person when I was married to him, as long as I let him do what he wanted. Having studied book illustration at The Art Students League, portrait painting and textile design at the School of Visual Arts, film and TV production at the New York Institute of Technology, and finally a degree in Interior Design at FIT, I was looking for a profession to earn a living. I new I had nothing to go out into the world with; as a wife and mother, I had no credit, no credit cards and no skills. Thank God I had that insight and I started working part time at Equitable Life Assurance for $6 per hour at age forty, got my first credit card and have worked from there. There were many ups and downs in the twenty-two years in the industry. I lost jobs due to corporate restructuring, resizing, down-sizing, re-engineering, market crash and survived it all on my own two feet. I had financial responsibilities and just kept going and it was no easy task. I was depressed in those days — you damn right, I was and there was no one I could borrow money from to eliminate the high pressure. It took eight years of working for me to be able to get divorced and relocated, as it was no light matter."

Later divorcing Hans, Catherine established herself in corporate design and planning for such companies as The Equitable, Merrill-Lynch and Heller Financial, purchased by GE Capital, Inc. in 2001. Now Catherine Buxhoeveden has traveled extensively yet chose to make her permanent home on Long Island's East End where she'd been vacationing for over twenty years. Buyers and sellers who work with Catherine gain not only from her world of knowledge, but her wealth of expertise in design, construction and real estate. Over two decades of proven business experience as an in-house project manager is brought to the table, which involved managing multi-construction and design projects, site selection and lease negotiations for local and regional offices of major companies. A South Hampton homeowner and resident, she has purchased and sold many of her own personal properties. Catherine's transition into residential sales in her hometown seemed a natural one. Her success and reputation, as a result, have been exceptional, and based on the key element of "listening to your client." Highly seasoned in the arts of effective negotiations, solution oriented service and spatial conception, she possesses all the right ingredients necessary to help discerning buyers and sellers accomplish all their real estate goals.

1948, Hans on a Bermuda Cruise.

Author's Reflection

As for Hans, I hope I was able to create a good impression of who Hans Holzer was and is. Who could possibly marry a ghost man and bear his children? Many things must be taken into account when dealing with the paranormal. It would take a strong connection for the two individuals I call my parents to become united as they were. I truly believe that the day they met there were unnatural forces at work. Perhaps a spiritual hand came down and gently prodded Catherine along to meet Hans through my late Aunt Rosemarie. Logically I would ask why then all the hoopla of my late aunt having had dated my father? Why not simply place Hans and Catherine together and be done with it! The answer to that question I have learned recently is that the Lord, or something, does work in mysterious and annoying ways at times. If people, places or things just placed together neatly like matching puzzle pieces then this would be a perfect, non-chaotic and clean world. Knowing that is not the case leaves one to ponder and ask more of one's own existence. My own conclusion is that in order for Hans and Catherine to meet there was a greater plan at work. A master plan that had nothing to do with any human being on earth. I feel it was from an unknown source that chooses not to reveal itself. I suppose the source wants to keep its affiliations private. I can respect that. When my sister and I came along, the marriage slowly began to fade. I often asked the questions as to why then were Hans and Catherine together in the first place?

Again, it wouldn't be until recently that I understood the answer. To have us silly! Nadine and I were born into his world to go on and do great things as our parents before us. To help others and try to live a good and decent life. Nadine places people in jobs and lives on the phone morning, noon and night to get them work. She has been doing this what seems like forever as it is her calling and her passion. A driving force behind her, pushing her when times are tough and money is tight. As for myself, the same ... but through my writing and love of literature. Becoming a paranormal expert has many prices to it. But the rewarding one outweighs any cynic, skeptic or eyebrow raiser. As a parent of four and having my hands in the pot, I will continue on regardless of anyone's stink eye. No matter if you're famous or not, as long as you are true to yourself and the ones you love, you can't go wrong. Even when things in life, do. Below is a brief summary of where us characters are now living in 2008 and trying to continue this process called life — learning, evolving, spiritual growth and accepting that we can't change the past but certainly can change our present. That's if we really want too. And if we can't just say that four letter word along with the word 'it' after, we can move on!

1960, Riverside Drive Apartment.

Catherine is still creating art as she is currently exhibiting at Guild Hall Museum in East Hampton from time to time and has some art used as covers for local magazines. She also does personal portraits for those who are trying to re-capture a loved one or pet that has passed. Though, she also draws the living, she mainly keeps to landscapes. Her partner and I have encouraged her to paint on a more spiritual level after the passing of Rosemarie. Catherine, through my own personal awakenings, has re-opened her "gift" and psychic abilities becoming more spiritual and relaxed. As life has hardened her and molded her into a cast of the woman she once was, I'd like to think I was able to slowly unwind her a bit through the past couple of years of my own turbulence. I feel that this was part of my own fate, as Hans before me, to help anyone in need on my path at the time. That it comes when it is the right time and not when we want it to. This is a lesson in life of patience and understanding. One I have yet to achieve as I am still young. However, Catherine has leant herself to becoming a more softer individual who is trying to find herself and ask why was she placed here? What is her sole purpose on this earth this time around? For all of us this is a personal and one of a kind question that only we can answer.

Dr. Daniel P. Buxhoeveden, (Uncle Danny), Research Associate Professor: He received his JD in Law from Loyola University in 1984 and his Ph.D. in Biological Anthropology from The University of Chicago in 1993. In 1995, he was awarded a McDonnell-Pew Foundation Fellowship to study Cognitive Science at the University California, San Diego. Daniel is interested in the reiterative micro-organization of the cortex and how this can be applied to comparative neuroscience, medicine, and brain evolution. Vertical micro-units are thought to be fundamental building blocks of the cortex, and recent evidence suggests these units are altered in selected regions of the cortex in certain neurological conditions and also prenatal cocaine exposure. He is currently pursing research grants on the effects of cocaine on developing vertical cell columns, autism, and comparative brain anatomy among primates. One interesting question is whether insults to these units from diverse sources, be it environmental or genetic, that are incurred during the critical phases of cortical development, result in similar organizational outcomes? If this is the case, then physiological changes to the units would be predictable while the behavioral outcomes would be dictated according to specificity of a given cortical region. This would provide a basic underlying principle to many diverse neurological conditions. Daniel is especially drawn to the significance of autistic spectrum disorders and other anomalies of the brain and mind in the context of the contemporary human

**1975, Nadine, Alexandra, and Catherine in
an Austrian Village.**

condition. Upon writing numerous sample papers on these topics, Daniel continues to pursue University's for grants and funding for his research. It is always an uphill battle for him but he is making great strides regardless.

In the end, he is doing a good thing for humanity and the world needs more like him. Some of the headers for his papers with whom he shared with others are: Accelerated maturation in brains of patients with Downs syndrome in the Journal of Intellectual Disability, Disruption in the inhibitory architecture of the cell mini column: implications for autism in The Neuroscientist. The mini column and evolution of the brain in Brain, behavior, and Evolution. Mini columnar pathology in Dyslexia in Annals of Neurology.

1971, Rosine and Hans at a hotel in Vienna, Austria.

The mini column hypothesis in neuroscience: A Review in Brain, behavior, and Evolution. Asperger's syndrome and cortical neuropathology in Journal of Child Neurology. Mini column pathology in autism in Neurology. © 2005 University of South Carolina Board of Trustees.

1983, Nadine and Alexandra, one of the many stressful Holzer dinners.

Rosine is still cooking her fabulous recipes and has passed them along to me and I surprise her with them at the holiday gatherings we host each year. She currently resides with Uncle Danny and his wife. I have since been in contact with her late mother with whom she really never knew. They are *all* coming since my late Aunt Rosemarie opened the floodgates. She loves it. I always look forward to hearing from her as her tiny but robust Parisian voice carries throughout my soul. I enjoy speaking in French with her, remarkably, still understanding my broken French. The last time I took a grammar lesson I was in eighth grade. But in her polite French way, she always seems to understand nonetheless. Sometimes she'll ask if I have any news from her mother as she is preparing herself mentally to cross over. I feel badly but understand that she lived a life of turmoil, love, war, loss, pain and looking back she just wants to go to the place where her family is. Including losing three out of her five children. Her psychic road has ended to where she has openly accepted her fate. If one believes in reincarnation then I would hope for either to be done, or to come back with no worries.

Nadine has put the volleyballs away for a career in sales and a family of her own. But, I suspect there are closet volleyballs somewhere in her apartment! She continues on in helping many in need of a job in the food services industry. A noble profession as her husband also places people but for a different industry.

Alexandra and Nadine celebrating Rosine's 81st Birthday.

As she continues on her own path of growth and development, her bumps in her road must work themselves out like anyone else. Knowing she has other interest perhaps may lead her down yet another path in her life. I mentioned Real Estate to her once as I had an impression, and she voiced out how much she would love to do that as well.

Perhaps one day she may find herself slowly weaving into that spot, as her life may yet again take another turn. One never truly knows what tomorrow will bring, and I assume that is why we have expressions like 'live for today for we know not what tomorrow brings' or 'live for the moment.'

As for myself, I am writing and fielding many projects at once, the usual chaos that I call my life. I feel comfortable writing about a world that does not exist until I make it so. A place that I would love to fly right into and land. Perhaps float around a bit and encounter a friendly ghost like casper when I was a child and loving that cartoon. Perhaps I could come across an undiscovered civilization where people were always friendly and respectful, and everyone was beautiful any time of the day. Of course I wouldn't want this new race to be that perfect, as it would get dull in a hurry. I would want some action and chaos mixed into my new world. But for now, on earth and in reality I am raising four children with my husband living outside of Manhattan. I am more spiritual and do believe that we are all on a path. It's just up to us which direction to go in. If we are difficult and choose the wrong way, we will eventually circle back around and go the right way. I am reminded of the scene from the movie, 'National Lampoon's European Vacation' where actor Chevy Chase' character just can't get left! If you'd like to learn more about Hans and his true ghost experiences and other paranormal events you can visit on line with using a search for his name. See his extensive library of titles on ghostly expeditions from around the globe, Amityville and anything supernatural to a few fictitious titles. You can choose a title or two that will transform your inner being to another world beyond ours. It was nice sharing this with with you and I do hope that you will keep reading what the Holzer's put out, enjoying them as much as we have enjoyed writing them. Caution: You may want to leave the lights on at night...if not for just awhile.

1980, Riverside Drive Apartment, Christmas with Rosine and Catherine.

1985, Hans in his Galley Style Kitchen.

Right:
1990, Hans.

1993, Christmas at Catherine's Apartment with Alexandra, Catherine and Nadine.

1982, Chester, New York: Hans attempting to play tennis once again.

1982, Chester, New York: Hans attempting to play tennis twice again.

Hans Holzer

Catherine Buxhoeveden

1972, Farm House Badase, Austria with Catherine, Nadine, Alexandra and Rosine.

Mid 1960s, Catherine in Ireland.

1971, Rosine, Catherine, and Alexandra in Bassinet, Vienna Park, Austria.

Right:
1971, Rosine, Catherine, and Alexandra
in Bassinet, Vienna Park, Austria.

1953, Ronkonkoma, Long Island: Alexander, Rosine, Theodore and Hans Kessler.

1973, Ronkonkoma, Long Island: Rosine and Hans.

1985, Patchogue, Long Island: Rosemarie, Catherine and Rosine at the tennis courts.

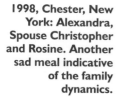

1998, Chester, New York: Alexandra, Spouse Christopher and Rosine. Another sad meal indicative of the family dynamics.

**September 1933, The Wedding Day. Rosine Claire Vidal
and Count Alexander Buxhoeveden.**

1969, Hans, Catherine and Nadine are at the Riverside Drive Apartment. Notice Catherine's haunted artwork in the background.

1975, Alexandra is shown in background as Hans displays his book, *The Habsburge Curse*, while at their Austrian Farm House.

1975, Catherine, Nadine and Alexandra in front of a cathedral in Austria.

Catherine's father, Count Alexander Buxhoeveden.

1976, Riverside Drive, New York: Hans, Rosine, Nadine and Alexandra.

1970, Riverside Drive Park, New York: Hans attempting to ride a bike.

1968, Riverside Drive Apartment: Hans and Catherine going to a charity event.

1966, Riverside Drive Apartment: Hans and his father, Leonard, and Nadine.

1975, Hans, Nadine, Catherine, and Alexandra at the tennis courts in Austria.

1969, Catherine inside the Buxhoeveden Church. Notice the family crest above her.

1946, Florence, Italy: Rosine with her four children. Top left Theodore and Alexander. Bottom left Rosemarie and Catherine.

1965, Rosine one last time with all five Buxhoeveden children. Left to right is Theodore, Rosemarie, Daniel, Catherine, Rosine and Alexander.

Bibliography

Belanger, Jeff. "Dr. Hans Holzer, A Lifetime of Explaining the Unexplained." Online article.

Brockway, Rev. Laurie Sue. "Ghost Buster." On-line article.

Henry of Lativia. "Albert of Riga." *Chronic of Livonia*.

Holzer, Hans. "Fifth Avenue Ghost." *Ghost Hunter*, 1964.

James, Gary. On-line interview.

Joyner, Charles. Newspaper clipping. *Wilmington Star News*. New Hanover County, Wilmington, North Carolina; 1964.

Kirk, Arnold. "German Bomb Once Threatened Countess." Wilmington, North Carolina, May 3, 1964.

Lowry, Maxine. "She Hunts Ghosts, Paints 'Em." *The New York World Telegram and Sun*, November 8, 1963.

"Man and the Machine: An Exhibit of Graphics." September 27-October 25, 1970.

Merlian News Articles. Merryn Jose, Publisher, Editor and Author

McHarry, Charles. "On the Town." The Daily News, December 5, 1963.

Moore, Clement. *The Night Before Christmas.*

New York Community Investigation of Paranormal Occurrences

New York Journal American, March 27, 1965,

Nickell, Joe. *Investigative Files for Ghost Hunters.*

Occultism and Parapsychology Encyclopedia.

Ploeg, Dirk Vander. "Interview with the Ghost Hunter." UFO Digest. com, August 2007.

Polier, Betsy. "Park East Art and Artists." September 30-October 13, 1966.

Shlachter, Barry. *The Associated Press.*

Tallmer, Jeremy. "At Home with Hans and Catherine Holzer." *New York Post*, March 15, 1975.